HEX WEAVE & MAD WEAVE

An Introduction to Triaxial Weaving

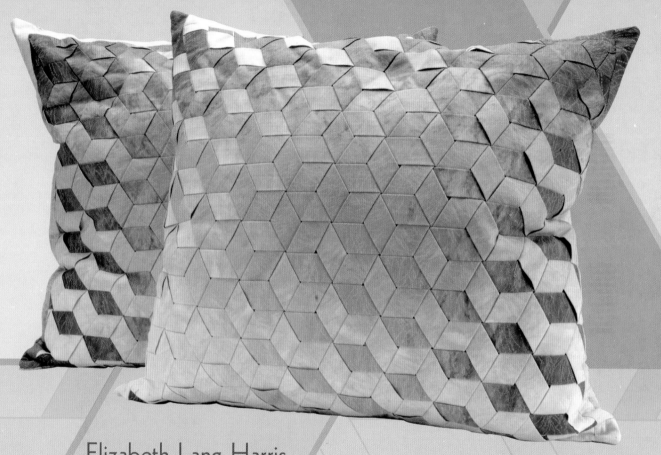

Elizabeth Lang-Harris
& Charlene St. John

Schiffer Publishing Ltd

4880 Lower Valley Road • Atglen, PA 19310

Other Schiffer Books on Related Subjects:
The Techniques and Art of Weaving: A Basic Guide
978-0-7643-4413-8, $34.99
Weaving A Chronicle, 978-0-7643-4063-5, $39.99
The Art of Weaving, 978-0-8874-0079-7, $34.95

Type set in Geometr231 BT/Geometr212 BT

ISBN: 978-0-7643-4465-7
Printed in China

Published by Schiffer Publishing, Ltd.
4880 Lower Valley Road
Atglen, PA 19310
Phone: (610) 593-1777; Fax: (610) 593-2002
E-mail: Info@schifferbooks.com

For our complete selection of fine books on this and related subjects, please visit our website at *www.schifferbooks.com*. You may also write for a free catalog.

This book may be purchased from the publisher. Please try your bookstore first.

We are always looking for people to write books on new and related subjects. If you have an idea for a book, please contact us at proposals@schifferbooks.com.

Schiffer Publishing's titles are available at special discounts for bulk purchases for sales promotions or premiums. Special editions, including personalized covers, corporate imprints, and excerpts can be created in large quantities for special needs. For more information, contact the publisher.

• IN DEDICATION TO SHEREEN LAPLANTZ •

CONTENTS

FOREWORD

Evidence of woven objects is ubiquitous and ancient. People have been weaving, both in two and three dimensions, for thousands and thousands of years. Basket forms have been carbon-dated at 10,000 to 12,000 years old, well before pottery arrived beside the cook fire. And the kind of triaxial weaves in this book were probably among the earliest weaves. Fragments of "hex" weave baskets have been found in archeological sites in Japan that date back 7,000 years. The point is that this book is not about something new. It is about rediscovery.

The urge to weave seems almost as elemental to human history as the use of fire. Who was the first weaver? I have always imagined that the very first baskets were made of intertwined fingers…a quick way to create a vessel to hold more berries than a single palm. But the human mind never rests and that one idea … creating something that would hold together by using the tension created by going in and out…a simple engineering principal…lead to the long history and deep traditions of basketry and weaving.

Triaxial weave is one of the oldest, most practical, and common. You find the triaxial weave everywhere. I have seen it hanging from a tree over the Orinoco River, covered in dust in Tanzania, and holding hotel soaps in Tokyo. Once you get the hang of it, it is a fast weave to produce sturdy vessels of any size. Like other basketry techniques, however, utility was never enough. Humans just seem to need to decorate everything.

Today's weavers and basket makers do not need to make useful objects. Plastic containers fit better in the refrigerator than ribbed egg baskets and modern looms chug out yards of cloth at dizzying speed.

But lots and lots of people still spin and weave and lots and lots of people still bang splints out of trees to make baskets. We may have outgrown our need to weave by hand, but we have not lost our fascination with the process and the products.

Many people find satisfaction in making things with their hands and love the challenge of making more and more complicated objects that challenge both their minds and coordination. For these people, for those who love a good puzzle, triaxial weaves are a thing of joy.

Triaxial weaves are not easy. I have taught hex weave and have observed a fair amount of lip-chewing and brow-furrowing. People wrestle with it and students eventually "get" it in unique ways, recognizing and duplicating the pattern in a way that works for them. Teaching triaxial weaves always gives me a profound appreciation for the many, many ways humans learn.

Clearly triaxial weaves are a source of joy and adventure to the authors of this book. Throughout history, techniques are rediscovered and reinvigorated by the curiosity and diligence of weavers like Elizabeth Harris and Charlene St. John. It has been over a decade since Elizabeth and I located one copy of Shereen LaPlantz's book, The Mad Weave Book, and tried to figure out how her directions meshed with the illustrations in Virginia Harvey's book, The Techniques of Basketry. The authors of this book are now part of a long and honorable chain of weavers, rediscovering this ancient weave and carrying it into the twenty-first century. Maintaining that link back to the thousands of years of basket making and weaving make their work and this book important.

By Lois Russell
President, National Basketry Organization

INTRODUCTION

Did you love plane geometry? Can you tessellate with the best? Are you addicted to origami? TRIAXIAL WEAVING COULD BE FOR YOU!

We had both been working with triaxial weaving for years before we met. When we finally did meet, we could not stop talking, waving our arms around, and drawing pictures on napkins. So, we decided to write a book. There isn't much written about triaxial weaving, and we wanted to share what we had learned about these intriguing weave structures and make them accessible to a wide variety of readers.

We invite weavers who have always enjoyed the extra dimension of supplemental warps and wefts, craftspeople who want more than squares and circles, quilters who are intrigued with Escher designs, paper artists looking for a new angle in approaching their two and three dimensional creations, and anyone intrigued with the art of tessellation to enter the world of triaxial weaving.

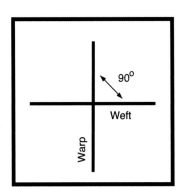

We typically use two axes in on-loom weaving: *warp* and *weft*. The vertical and horizontal axes meet at 90°. This is a biaxial drawing; it has two axes.

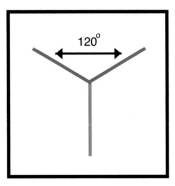

Triaxial weaves have three axes that meet at 120°.

Our approach to triaxial weaving draws from two traditions: the single-colored hex weave and mad-weave baskets made in many cultures throughout the world, and mosaic tiling, which is not weaving at all, but is the study of patterns on a surface.

We move in a world of 90° corners, or a biaxial world. However, the basic figure in triaxial weaving is the triangle. We will be working with a particular kind of triangle, the equilateral triangle, which has three sides of identical length and three interior angles of 60°.

Now, suppose we add a second warp or weft and change the orientation of the axes so that they meet at a 120° angle. There are great increases in patterning and color interaction. Triaxial means "three axes." Triaxial weaves use three elements that intersect at 120°.

Fabric or paper woven in triaxial weaves are very strong and have no bias. The consequence of the triangle's strength is that both hex weave and mad weave are quite stiff and do not drape well. As you start dreaming over projects to make, avoid using mad weave or hex weave for things that have to bend, like elbows!

It is difficult to weave a triaxial weave on a biaxial loom. It can be done, however, and is a topic for a more advanced study. The focus of this first book is on two of the simplest triaxial weaves, the "hexagonal" or "hex" weave, which is the triaxial equivalent of the biaxial tabby and "mad weave," which is the equivalent of a biaxial twill. We will weave these simple structures off-loom.

We wrote Hex Weave & Mad Weave: An Introduction to Triaxial Weaving, as the starting point for anyone in interested in triaxial weaving. We expect many people will want to show off their new skills as they master these intriguing weaves, so we have included "quick start" projects with some of the sections. We take you step-by-step through the process as you construct a quick, but usable weaving. In addition, there are more challenging projects described in detail placed near the topics they illustrate. There are suggestions about record-keeping and the beginning of a pattern library.

The concepts and techniques are not difficult, and the many diagrams of constructing hex and mad weaves reflect the difficulty we sometimes encounter when we try to write in words what we could demonstrate in seconds.

We suggest that you begin with hex weave and work through the book in order. The projects get more complicated as you go along, and the project assumes that you already know the material before it. But, if you are an experienced mad weave enthusiast, you can go directly to the woven-style section.

Mad weave has a bad reputation. Legend has it that mad weave is so difficult that putting it together drives the weaver mad. Not so. By the end of this book, you will have learned two different ways of weaving: both mad weave and hex weave, mad weave's older sibling, and when you say "I am mad about mad weave" … it will be with a smile.

By Elizabeth Lang-Harris and Charlene St. John

HEX WEAVE
1:MATERIALS

⬤ WORKING WITH PAPER

Paper is an excellent medium for constructing triaxial weaves. There are beautiful papers available commercially, and you probably have scores of free papers that pass through your mailbox in the form of cards, catalogs, and calendars. You can paint heavy paper with acrylic or watercolor paints, immersion-dye paper in dyes used for plant fibers, and you can print out your own designs using paint programs on your computer.

Supplies

Most of the supplies we need for weaving hex weave and mad weave are commonplace household items or are relatively inexpensive and easily obtained.

◊ HEAVY PAPER (card stock or heavier to cut into strips or used for backing.) Heavy scrap-booking paper is ideal. It comes in twelve-inch squares, and strips that are one-quarter of an inch wide and twelve inches long are a good size for the projects in this book. The papers may be patterned or textured. Try other papers, too.

◊ PAPER-CUTTING TOOLS (one or more of the following:)

- Scissors used only for paper. (Paper dulls the blades of scissors and it becomes difficult to use them for cutting fabric.)
- Paper cutters and trimmers, either rotary or guillotine.
- Paper shredders: NOT the kind that only cross-cut.
- Pasta machines. The old hand-cranked machines can often be found in yard sales and thrift shops.
- Handheld rotary cutter and mat (such as Olfa®)
- Rag rug cutter

◊ STORAGE COMPARTMENTS for organizing and storing extra paper strips. I make long envelopes from scrap-booking paper or large calendar pages.

◊ WORK SURFACE. The work surface should be stiff and sturdy. It should not be slippery, but have some texture to help keep the strips in place. It would be helpful if it could rotate or be moved easily, and a useful size for most projects is about 15" by 15". If you only have access to a slippery surface, you may need to pin or tape one or both ends of the strips to keep them put. Feel free to improvise.

◊ PINS, TAPE, OR WEIGHTS to hold the strips to the work surface.

◊ GLUE to fasten the ends of the strips after you have finished weaving.

◊ PENCILS for marking cutting lines.

◊ A LIFTER. Any small tool that can wiggle through layers of paper strips. You probably have many small implements around the house that would work. For example, you might try basketry tools, fine knitting needles, or tweezers.

○ PAINTS AND INEXPENSIVE BRUSHES for touch-ups or coloring the edges. If you have painted and then cut the paper, the edges are likely to be white. If you don't want white edges, then cut the strips, stack them together, and, with an almost dry brush, run the brush down over the edges of the strips until they are the color you want. Foam brushes work better because they don't have little bristles that splay out and paint whatever they encounter.

Finishing

It is a good thing to varnish your paper projects. I use acrylic varnish, both spray and liquid. Varnishing is particularly important for computer-printed papers since they have a tendency to run. Use the spray first, then paint several coats of varnish on the finished piece. The colors will intensify, and sometimes glow. Your piece will be water-resistant, but not do not immerse it. Wipe it clean with a damp cloth.

● WORKING WITH FABRIC

Cotton fabric intended for quilting is a good place to begin, but you can use almost any fabric that doesn't fray or fall apart with handling. You can make a small triangular pillow front with 3 or 4 fat quarters.

Fabric generally is not as stiff as heavy paper, so you will need something to fasten it to in order to put a little tension on the strips as you weave. Some examples:

- A rug onto which you can pin the fabric.
- A large embroidery hoop or embroidery frame.
- Foam core board
- Cork
- My personal favorite: A frame made of stretcher bars (the kind that painters use for stretching canvasses) to which I staple the ends of the fabric. I can see and reach both the front and back of the weaving. You can purchase them at most art stores and many craft-supply stores as well. Look for bars that have grooves that slide together so that you can make a triangular shape. You only need three bars for some projects, but buy four, so that you can also use them

for rectangular projects. You can reuse the bars many times. Twenty to twenty-four inches long is ideal.
- You may also have other triangular structures that you can use, such as an adjustable triangular weaving loom.

Supplies

As with the paper supplies, most of these supplies are common household items, but can also be purchased rather inexpensively.

○ SEWING TOOLS, plus a tool that lets you turn a tube of fabric inside-out

○ SEWING MACHINE (a very basic one will do)

○ FABRIC SCISSORS

○ BATTING for stuffing fabric tubes

○ STEAM IRON

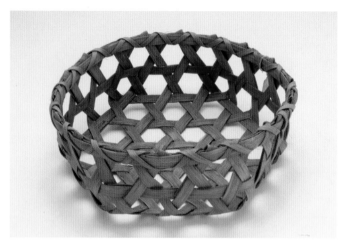

Contemporary rustic hexagonal-weave basket, c. 1980, 11" x 4".
Courtesy of Richard and Sukey Harri.

Thirty years later... and still in great shape!

Hexagonal, or hex weave is the simplest triaxial weave, with a tabby structure and a look of lace. Hex weave is a very old basket structure that is found throughout the world. It produces sturdy, versatile containers that can be used for many household tasks such as sifting, rinsing, and drying. Most of these baskets were woven in a single color and were purely functional. Although basket structures are the oldest form of hex weave, we will be focusing on the many two-dimensional structures that have succeeded it.

Today, hex weave is coming into its own. Type the words "hexagonal weave" into your Internet browser and you will find pages and pages of information. Hex weave is widely used in manufacturing, especially in the construction of strong, durable cloth. It is also of academic interest, especially in situations where you can combine art and mathematics, and, of course, artists are producing beautiful objects ranging from delicate jewelry to large wall pieces involving all forms of media from silk thread to metal.

There are many ways to construct hex weave. We want to show you our two favorites. The first, or radial, method, begins at the center of the hex weave and grows outwards from the center. The layered method begins with the horizontal elements all laid out before any weaving begins. We'll begin with the radial method.

✳ RADIAL HEX WEAVE

Radial hex weave has four components:

- RIGHT-POINTING STRIPS. The strips begin at the lower left and move upwards to the right.
- LEFT-POINTING STRIPS. These strips begin at the lower right and move upwards to the left.
- HORIZONTAL STRIPS.
- SPACE ENCLOSED WITHIN THE STRIPS.

The strips define the outline of the figure, leaving the inside free to be filled by whatever you choose. It is this flexibility makes hex weave so intriguing!

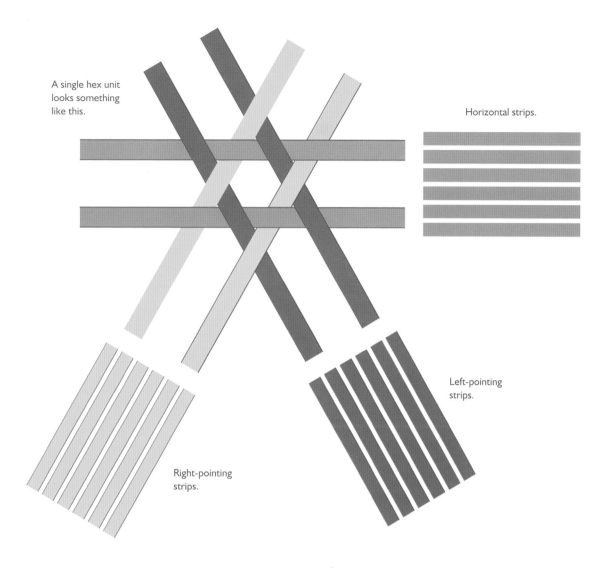

A single hex unit looks something like this.

Horizontal strips.

Left-pointing strips.

Right-pointing strips.

The six little holes, or triangles, that surround the central hexagon open space are the places where the three components meet. The size of the holes varies. It is largest when you are using inflexible strips, and may almost entirely disappear with fine ribbon.

Presence or absence of holes in the little triangles is not necessarily either bad or good. It offers us another design option. Increasing the size of the holes creates a lacier fabric. It also gives us the option to add another color without it being really noticeable. Holes can add a flash of another color if you back your weaving with colored paper or foils.

The hex unit on the left was formed using narrow, somewhat inflexible, figured wood veneer. The triangles are very large. The hex unit on the right was made from scrapbook-weight paper, and the holes are barely distinguishable. Both samples are about three inches point-to-point.

❋ STARS

In this project, we will make a small radial hex weave with two strips of paper in each direction (remember, there are three directions, so you will need a total of six strips of paper, about 1/4"-wide and 12" long). This beginning hex weave project uses one color per direction so that you can have an extra visual aid in placing the strips. Once you are comfortable with building hex weaves you will be able use as many colors as you choose, or use a single color throughout.

Supplies

- Two strips of color "A" to use as right-pointing strips.
- Two strips of color "B" to use as left-pointing strips.
- Two strips of color "C" to use as horizontal strips.
- A Work Surface.
- Pins, tape, or weights to hold the strips to the work surface.
- Glue to fasten the ends of the strips after you have finished weaving.
- Paper-cutting Scissors.

For more information about supplies, see Chapter One.

Construction

○ STEP 1: Begin with two strips, a right-pointing strip and a left-pointing strip, and cross them in the middle, with about 60 degrees between them. If you have the right-pointing strip on top, you are beginning a right-handed hex. Most hex weaves are left-handed, but I believe that once you are building hexes with speed, it is more comfortable to use right-handed hexes. Once you have chosen the direction of the first cross, you must continue to weave in that same direction.

○ STEP 2: Now add the third element — the horizontal strip. This completes the first triangle. Place the horizontal strip between the arms of the right- and left-pointing strips, which locks it in place. Gently tighten the three strips, but do not try to stretch them or to force them together.

IMPORTANT!

Hex weave always uses the same weave structure regardless of the medium in which it is woven. The most delicate jewelry and the largest sculpture share the same structure, so, once you have mastered the techniques below, you are ready to plow new ground.

STEP 1

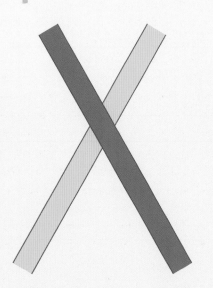

Right cross. The right-pointing strip moves up to the right and passes over the left-pointing strip.

Left cross. The left-pointing strip travels over the right-pointing strip.

Step 2

The basic triangle, right-handed.

The basic triangle, left-handed.

All of the intersections are right-pointing. No matter how you turn the triangle, the pattern is the same. The right-pointing strip always travels under the horizontal strip and over the left-pointing strip. You will see these little triangles in each intersection of strips in both hex and mad weaves, and they all have the same structure.

For the rest of this chapter, we will work only with right-handed constructions. If you prefer using left-handed hex weaves, reverse the directions, so that "weave under the left-facing strips" becomes "weave under the right-facing strips." The steps will be the same, but the directions will be reversed.

We said earlier that hex weave is the plain weave, or tabby of triaxial weaving. We can see that each individual strip alternates going over or under each successive strip. This is important enough that it merits a name. The "Plain Weave Rule" says that in a finished hex weave, all of the components follow a plain weave pattern, "over one, under one, over one, under one…." There will be times when it is faster to break the pattern when weaving, especially at the edges, but at the end all strips should be put in order.

You may have already encountered the plain weave rule. If your first try at inserting the horizontal strip resulted in the horizontal strip just sliding through the cross, you are likely to have lost your tabby structure. Remove the horizontal strip and check the direction of the basic cross.

Adding strips four, five, and six is a little awkward because there is not a lot to keep the new strips anchored. You may want to fasten or weigh down the ends of the strips to keep everything in place.

◇ STEP 3: The fourth strip is easy. Put a second horizontal strip on the other side of the basic cross, and parallel to the first horizontal strip. From here onward, in the diagrams, the strip that was just added will be colored green so it will be easy to identify.

◇ STEP 4: Now add the fifth strip, which is left-pointing. It takes the same path as the first left-pointing strip, traveling over the horizontal strips and under the right-pointing strip. But there is a problem: the violation of the plain weave rule. The lower halves of both left-leaning strips are next to each other, floating over the lower horizontal line. This is easily corrected: just switch the order of the last two strips so that the bottom of the green left strip is beneath the lower red horizontal strip, rather than on top of it.

(Steps 3, 4, and 5 are pictured on following page)

IMPORTANT!

After adding each strip, check the new strip to make sure that it hasn't broken the plan weave rule. This is most common for the strips at either end of the insertion, and are no problem if you catch them early.

STEP 3

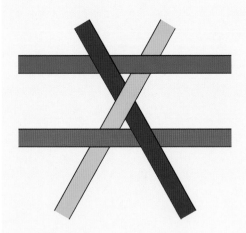

Hex weave after adding the fourth strip.

STEP 4

Hex weave after adding the fifth strip.

STEP 5

Hex weave after adding the sixth strip.

◇ STEP 5: The sixth strip is a second right-pointing strip. You now have two strips in each direction. The whole thing may be out of alignment, so this is a good time to restore order. You want to see a small hexagonal hole in the center, and all right-pointing strips should be parallel, all left-pointing strips should be parallel, all horizontal strips should be parallel.

Congratulations! You have just completed weaving the basic hex weave star. These are fun to make and to give. Make them in different colors and sizes, use them singly or in groups that dance across the page. The most obvious use for these little charmers is to enhance handmade cards, but they can also be ornaments. Color both sides and make tiny, tiny earrings (glue and varnish both sides, and they will be beautiful for years) or go in the other direction and make the star large enough to hold an announcement or invitation. Note: We have not yet finished the edges, so your star will look as if it has tentacles. We will get to edgings later in this chapter.

✳ MULTIPLE RADIAL HEX UNITS

Constructing multiple hex units is an extension of making a single unit. After placing strip six to complete your first hex unit, you just keep going.

I have shown the addition of strips seven, eight, and nine (see drawings at top of next page). I usually turn the project with each new strip added so that I am inserting strips from the same orientation. This helps to keep my tension uniform. I prefer working from the top because is easier to pull strips down than to push them up. Do whatever feels more comfortable to you.

Look at what is happening in the middle of each green strip. Assuming that you are moving around the hex weave in a regular order, every third strip you add, beginning with the fourth strip, will not violate the plain weave rule. It will simply sit, cradled in the space between the left-pointing and right pointing strips. Every first and second strip you add will create at least one place in the middle of the new strip where the new strip intersects the other hex components to form a small triangle. Each time this happens there is a violation of the plain weave rule until you lock in the new strip by crossing the two others over the new one. We saw this when we added strips four, five, and six.

Hex weave after adding the seventh strip.   Hex weave after adding the eighth strip.   Hex weave after adding the ninth strip.

Here is another example. Look at the top horizontal strip of the hex weave below and you will see three interesting events: The two strips in the middle of the top row, right-pointing (yellow) and left-pointing, (blue) have just crossed the newly added horizontal red strip, which helps lock the new strip in place.

Most of the mistakes in weaving hex weave come at the ends. Here we see that both the second and third blue strips are traveling over the top red strip, violating the plain weave rule. This is easily fixed by exchanging the ends of the red strip and the third blue strip. On the other side of the red strip, two yellow strips have fallen under

the red. Again, this is fixed easily by just switching the unwoven ends of the red strip and the yellow.

If you find that there are places in the middle of the new strip where you do not have plain weave, it is likely that all you have to do is exchange the positions of one or more pre-existing strips. Raise the free ends of the two strips and then gently cross, or exchange, the tops. The already-woven sections are not affected. Think of the new strip as a fence and that half of your friends are on one side and the other half are on the other. People pair off — one from each side of the fence. They lock arms, which keeps the fence in place.

Placing Strips

There are a number of ways that you can insert the strips. It is slower but less error-prone to enter strips from the side of the row, beginning at one end and moving over and under each successive strip. The existing strips move very little, and the new strip snakes through the unwoven strips. It is faster, but more error-prone, to work from the loose ends of the web itself. Here the new strip is held fairly straight, and enters from the top. The existing ends are manually lifted, and the new stripped is slipped in.

Your way of entering strips and turning the working surface may result in no violations of the plain weave rule other than the one crossover in the middle of the row, if that. You are probably doing a perfect job in preparing each row before you weave.

This hex weave shows ways in which you can violate the plain-weave rule.

13

Angle Guide

As you are weaving, you will find that the angles tend to fluctuate. Paper and ribbon move quite freely, and you will have to straighten the hex frequently, especially at the beginning when there is not enough friction to hold the strips in place.

Once your project has become larger and more stable, you can check your angles less frequently, but, for now, if you see any distortion of the pattern, check your angles. You can use this guide to monitor angles.

To use the angle guide, lay it on top of your hex weave with the bottom line of your guide lined up with one of your strips. The other two dimensions of your hex should be aligned pretty closely to the arms of the guide.

You are welcome to copy the angle guide and use it at whatever size is helpful. You might want to mount it on a heavy background or even draw it directly on to your triaxial weaving work surface.

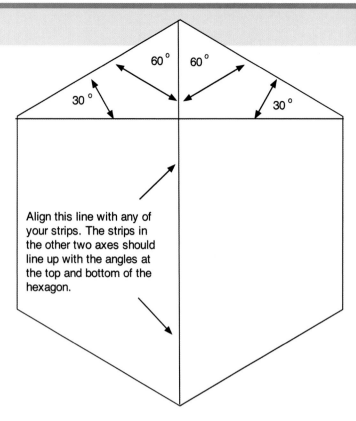

Align this line with any of your strips. The strips in the other two axes should line up with the angles at the top and bottom of the hexagon.

QUICK START PROJECT

❄ EDGES

This project comes in three parts. First, you will make four 2 x 2 x 2 hex layers (remember that a 2 x 2 x 2 hex has two strips on each of its six sides.) Then you will finish the hex weaves by using four different edge finishes. In the third step, you will assemble the hexes into little mobiles.

If you are working with paper or some other medium that has stable edges and ends, you will probably glue the pieces together and cut off the excess ends. There are many ways to cut and glue, giving you some design tools that are more difficult or impossible to duplicate in other materials. You will probably want to develop a library of decorative edgings. We will start with my four favorites.

The three paper trees were made using holiday cards cut into strips and vintage buttons. All three trees are about 7" long, exclusive of fringe.

Four Basic Edgings

1) Bare Bones Edging

Cut off everything that extends beyond the sides of the hexagon so that there is no decorative edging, then glue down each strip. This treatment produces the smallest hex, with the focus on the center. It is also the sturdiest edging.

2) Small Points Edging

The small-points example is a second small hexagon made from twelve one-quarter inch strips. The points are essentially free — you don't need any more strips than does the bare bones example, just slightly longer strips. It is easier to finish than the bare bones example.

Moving all around the outside of the weaving, pair the end of each strip with the end of a second strip on the other side of the fence (horizontal strip). Cross the two strips and move to the next pair. When all the pairs have been crossed, glue each pair where they overlap, and cut off the lose ends. This edging is simple to do, and wears well.

3) Fancy Points Edging

Instead of overlapping the ends, and cutting them into points, cut the strips so that they extend beyond their intersection. They are glued together at their intersection. This edging is not as sturdy as the first two because the "fringe" is only one layer thick. However, if you are going to glue down the piece, or put it where it will not be handled, it will be fine. It is the second-largest of these four edgings.

4) Large Points Edging

This is an important edging that adds some variation in scale to the weave. The long diagonal points appear at the corners of a multi-unit hex and are formed by incomplete hex units. You will see these come and go as you are working. Pay attention to them — they are particularly useful when you are designing with hex weave.

The large points still need only twelve strips. The sample has six large points, one at each corner of the multi-unit hexagon. This is the largest of the edgings shown.

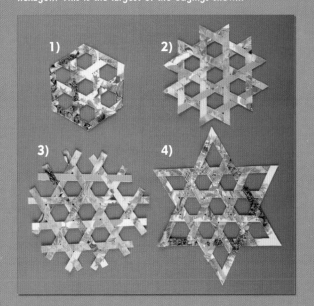

Supplies

- ◆ FORTY-EIGHT STRIPS OF PAPER (twelve strips each for four layers): Cut to about 1/4" x 8". Use heavy paper. Also, feel free to mix any colors or patterns that appeal to you.
- ◆ STRONG, HEAVY THREAD for stringing, about 30" long.
- ◆ NEEDLES FOR STRINGING.
- ◆ EIGHT BUTTONS FOR STRINGING: The buttons need to be big enough so that they won't fall through the center hole of the hexes. Their purpose is to separate and stabilize the layers. Remember that the holes have to be big enough to fit two strands of stringing cord. Buttons with buttonholes work better than shank buttons. You may want to make the layers before purchasing the buttons.

TIP:

If your weaving is big enough, you can combine different styles in one piece. You will soon find yourself designing your own edgings!

Instructions for Paper Mobiles

◯ STEP 1: Divide your strips into four groups of twelve strips each.

◯ STEP 2: Following the edging examples for finishing paper edges, make four 2 x 2 x 2 hex weaves, each with a different edging. Arrange the completed hex weaves by size.

◯ STEP 3: Fold your cord in half, so that you have two lengths of thread. Do not cut the thread!

◯ STEP 4: Using an overhand knot (not a slip knot) make a one-inch loop at the center of the cord. This loop will be used to hang the mobile. The cord now has a loop, a knot, and about thirteen inches of tail.

() STEP 5: String the tree from the top. Begin by stringing the top button, which could be a "showpiece" button, on the cord, putting each of the two ends through a different buttonhole. Tie a tight knot right up against the button. Follow the button with the smallest layer of hex weave, the one with the bare-bones edging. Put a large button and a knot after the hex layer to keep the hex weave stable and less likely to drop off to a lower layer. Leave about an inch and a half of unknotted cord, then repeat the instructions until you have used all the hex layers. It is much easier to put the mobile together using buttons that have holes rather than shank buttons.

() STEP 6: Don't forget to add a bottom button and a secure knot below it. Use the ends of the ribbon as fringe, or add a tassel.

() STEP 7: Hang the tree in your window!

The paper trees are light and lively, and the way that the layers move and change planes can be charming. Experiment with the number of layers and arrangement of colors. Try painting the undersides of the strips. Use beads instead of buttons. Stop the hex layers from slipping around and tilting.

🐝 FIGURED VENEER

The marquetry pieces were a wonderful surprise. I often use narrow strips of figured inlay banding as edgings for items I am going to frame. It is difficult to work with; it is brittle and much of the time can't be mitered successfully because little pieces start falling out of it.

However, I have found some highly patterned strips of wood inlay that are beautiful and surprisingly flexible. (See the Sources Page in the Appendix.) By oiling the strips before cutting them, and putting a drop of wood glue on the spot where you will cut — and also putting a drop of glue on the end of the fresh cut — the strips are flexible enough to make small projects.

The two samples pictured below are made of wood inlay. The simple three-star mobile hangs gracefully even with minimal weight at the bottom. The four-tier bush was made similarly to the project you just completed, but used single hex units. You can see the single-unit hexes of the little bush, the fancy point edging, spacers that give it more support, and, if you look under the top layer, you can see some bracing added to support the layers.

Don't be afraid to experiment. Almost anything that is flexible can be woven.

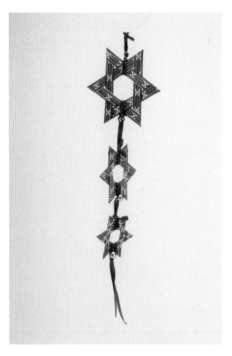

Three single marquetry stars are attached by ribbon, lightly weighted and suspended by the ribbon. Size: 4" wide, 14" long.

A little marquetry bush, 3" x 4".

Another view of the little marquetry hanging, showing the structure more clearly.

HEX FACTS

This chapter has focused on the basics of hex weave. Now that you have been thinking about hexagons and hex weaving, here are some interesting facts about hexes:

- Six equilateral triangles can fit into a hexagon sort of like a six-piece pizza. If the triangles are properly sized, they will cover the hexagon entirely. This relationship is called tiling the plane, or tessellation, and among the regular polygons, only triangles, squares, and hexagons can completely cover a flat surface alone.

- The distance between two of the flat walls across from each other in a hexagon is only about eighty-seven percent of the distance between two points opposite from each other.

- The rows in a multiple hex figure are not stacked right above each other. Each row moves over one-half of a hex and down a half – unit so that it fits snugly against the previous row. Weavers call this pattern a "diaper pattern."

- The size of a hex unit is determined by the width of the strips. A hex unit is a little more than three times the width of the strips from which it was constructed. When we get to mad weave, you will learn that it is a three-strip pattern and the hexagonal space in the center will be filled with two additional strips of the same width as the first.

If you have followed the text and done the projects in
this chapter, you are ready to begin designing!

HEX WEAVE
3: DESIGNING WITH HEXAGONS

The Quick Start project in the last chapter was to construct a star. In this chapter, we will create a variety of shapes, and you will learn how to design your own shapes.

Strip Calculator

This handy little table tells you how many strips you need to construct a regular hexagon if you specify either the number of hex units you want or the number of strips per side.

Each time you travel around the hexagon, adding one strip to each side of the hexagon, you are adding six strips to the total number of strips. This makes sense — hexagons have six sides!

HEX UNITS/SIDE	STRIPS/SIDE	TOTAL # OF STRIPS
1x1x1	2	6
2x2x2	4	12
3x3x3	6	18
4x4x4	8	24
5x5x5	10	30
6x6x6	12	36
7x7x7	14	42
8x8x8	16	48
9x9x9	18	54

Hex units can be made to look like a circle or they can approximate a polygon. Let's look at some of the shapes.

❀ ROUNDED FORMS

We begin with a hexagon. It takes six strips to construct, two each of the three basic strips (left-pointing, right-pointing, and horizontal). Note that with this exception of a drawing of a single hex unit, I have trimmed the extraneous loose ends from the edges of the drawings in this section (see figures next page). The actual hex unit really looks more like the figure on the right (ignore the colors for now).

A regular hexagon is longer from point to point than from wall to wall. The distance from wall to wall is approximately eighty-seven percent of the distance from corner to corner.

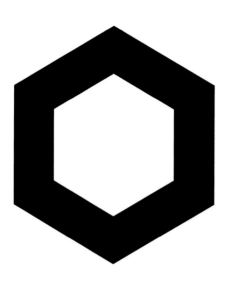

Hexagons are the basic building unit of hex weave.

Untrimmed hex unit.

Simple ball or flower shape.

Hex Weave 2 x 2 x 2

If you surround the single hex unit with six more hex units, the form appears more circular. It is a regular figure, a 2 x 2 x 2 multiple hex with two hex units per side. Think of this little hex weave as a basic flower shape — or you may see it as a ball or a balloon. This shape requires twelve strips, or four strips per direction.

Transition shape between a 2 x 2 x 2 hex and a 3 x 3 x 3 hex.

Transition Shapes

If you add yet another ring of six hexes, the weaving looks even more like a star or flower — today, though, it looks to me like a turtle. You need to add another six strips for this shape, for a total of eighteen strips.

It is easy to see images in the hex units. As we make our projects bigger, the images also get more complex.

This 3x3x3 Hex is rounded and is a versatile shape.

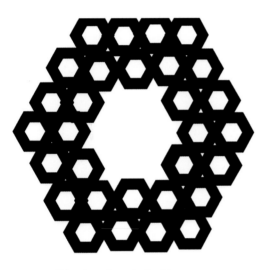

Wreath cut from 4 x 4 x 4 hex weave.

With eighteen strips, you can also complete the "turtle" figure above to a 3 x 3 x 3 hex. This is a good-sized hex and will look quite round, so it is a good choice for a ball or balloon, or a clock face, or the ice cream in an ice-cream cone.

The reason that this figure and the hex weave before it require the same number of strips is that the turtle is a cut-out of the 3 x 3 x 3 hex. In order to get the turtle shape, you have to weave a 3 x 3 x 3 figure and cut parts of it out. More cut-outs later.

Cutting Shapes

You can cut shapes from sheets of hex weave. This form, made of a 4 x 4 x 4 sheet of hexes, makes an attractive wreath. (Make certain that the strips in the original hex weave are securely glued, or some will fall out when you cut!)

We will return to curved figures shortly, but first, let's construct some angular forms.

♣ SHAPING ANGULAR FORMS

When we fashion shapes from hex weave using the radial method, we get a form that looks rounded. But what if we wanted a rectangular form, say four hex units on a side and ten hexes long? We would build a 4 x 4 x 4 hex weave, then stop adding strips to four of the sides and keep weaving on the other two until they have ten hex units. It looks like a fuzzy caterpillar before it is trimmed. After the loose ends are gone, it looks like a very squashed hexagon, which it is!

If you want the figure to look like a rectangle, the pointy ends of the figure have to go. You can get rid of them by cutting them off. You will have to cut through hex units, so be sure that you have glued thoroughly so that no little loose ends will fall out. Another option is to add units to the pointy ends until you approximate a straight line. There will always be a slightly wavy line because each successive line moves over half a hex unit.

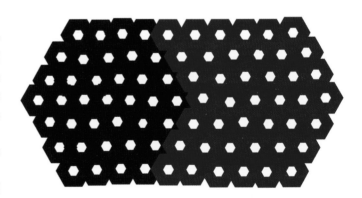

The original 4 x 4 x 4 rounded form is in blue. The magenta hex units were added to complete the form.

Small Rectangular Shapes

Hexagons can be used to construct images that are not circular in form. You can also create other angular forms in hex weave.

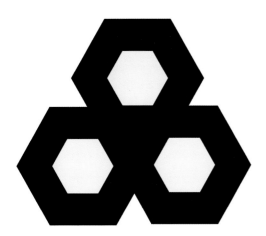

This is the simplest triangle. Beginning again with the basic hexagon, add two more hex units to make the simplest triangle. This triangle requires only nine strips.

Triangle composed of six hex units. I have added another layer at the bottom for a stronger triangle. This form is great for trees.

Two triangles make a diamond or a kite. Turn a three-unit triangle upside down and add it to the six-unit triangle. Now you have a diamond, or you can add a tail to make a kite. Let's add some color.

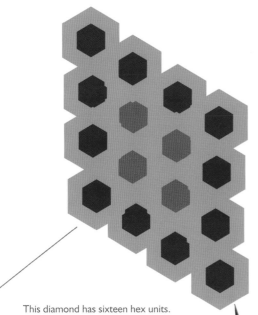

This diamond has sixteen hex units. As you would expect, the greater the number of hex units, the better the resolution of the diamond. The little bow will turn out to be very useful for embellishing. Try making several in different sizes and stacking them to make flowers or complex bows.

The bow for the kite's tail. The little bows on the kite can be made by placing two single-unit hexes next to each other. With their flat sides on the ground and a flat side on top, the units can be made to look like little rectangles. You may have to squint a little to ignore some of the deviations from rectangularity, but you can build up long chains of single-unit hexes.

Stacking

You can also build up approximations to rectangles by stacking rectangular rows. There are two ways of stacking: the first approach alternates wider and narrower rows, while the second form is "snake-form stacking." In the first method, the number of hexes per row varies, but the stack itself does not move more than one-half of a hex unit to the right or left. The image is stable and relatively static. In snake-form stacking, the number of hexes per row remains constant and you have a choice of moving half a hex unit to the right or left with each row. This is a much more dynamic image.

The rectangular approximations look more rectangular as the scale gets smaller, when there are a greater number of rows, and when the rows are wider.

Snake-form stacking.

This way of stacking, where the rows do not change position but get wider or narrower, is relatively static.

❦ COMPOUND FIGURES, COMBINING FORMS

The black and white pictures in the earlier part of this chapter gave you some basic building blocks. We will look at some colorful examples of combining forms and cutting out figures, and then play with a design project of your own.

The ice cream cone (black raspberry) composed of a 3 x 3 x 3 rounded form and a ten-hex triangular shape. The open centers of the ice-cream cone could be filled with almost endless possibilities for embellishment. However, eating the cone in this condition would be fraught with dripping. Let's add a background …

… That's better! There is no reason that the hex cells have to be empty. The filled ice-cream cone could be as simple as slipping two pieces of colored paper under the cone and under the ice cream.

Hearts

Templates for large and small hearts, to put in your pattern library, have been provide here. You are welcome to use or modify any of the patterns you see in this book.

Large Heart. This heart is another combination of rounded and angular figures: Do you see the two 2 x 2 x 2 hex weaves at the top of the heart? They are sitting on an upside down triangle that is balanced on its nose.

Small heart.

Mixed Media

Combining hex weave with other fiber and fabric techniques can be very effective. It would be difficult (but not impossible) to make the candles and flames using hex weave. The candlesticks, the candles, and the flame could each be a different color and/or texture: Embroider the flames in flame-stitch! Make the candles from short pieces of basket reed and wax them! Weave the candlestick holder from leather!

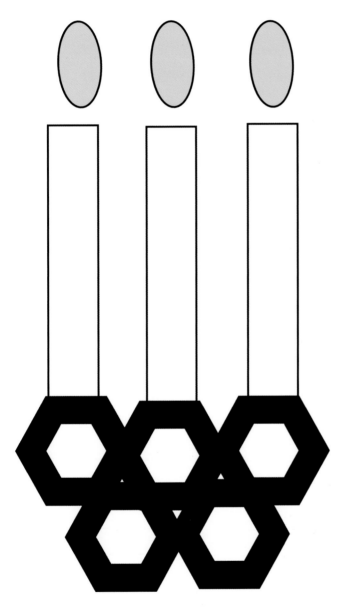

The candlestick is ready for embellishment.

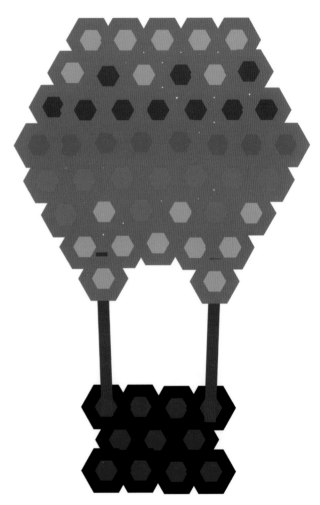

The sky's the limit! Here is a hot air balloon ready to take off. It started with a 5 x 5 x 5 rounded form and a 4 x 3 x 4 rectangular form. It also invites embellishments.

DESIGNING HEX-WEAVE EMBELLISHED ACCORDION JOURNALS

Accordion books are fun to make and fun to use, and even more fun to give. When you untie the ribbon that holds the book together, the book opens like an accordion or a concertina. This is definitely a book for the non-linear; you can go in any direction in whatever order you want!

Building an Accordion book begins with planning a hex design that will be glued to the cover. The cover is made by gluing a background paper to a very stiff piece of cardboard. Pick a paper that is compatible with the paper you are using for the figure since you will definitely see the background paper through the windows of the hex weave. After we have made the covers, we will make the accordion pages using two simple origami folds. Then we will have the fun of assembling the whole thing!

This may seem like a complicated project, but it's not. Take it one step at a time. I will walk you through it, let's put what you have just learned about designing into making your own, one-of-a kind figures from sheets of woven hex.

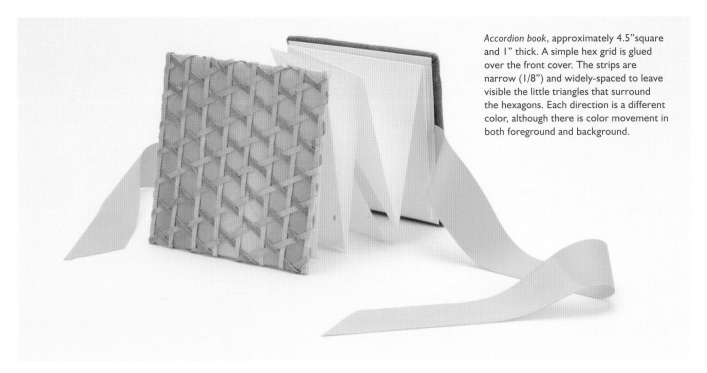

Accordion book, approximately 4.5"square and 1" thick. A simple hex grid is glued over the front cover. The strips are narrow (1/8") and widely-spaced to leave visible the little triangles that surround the hexagons. Each direction is a different color, although there is color movement in both foreground and background.

Supplies

- BEAUTIFUL PAPER for the background to your hex figure. A 12" x 12" piece will do. The paper should have some body, such as greeting cards, heavy patterned designer papers used in scrap-book making, or for people who like to paint their own papers, ninety- or one-hundred-and-forty pound watercolor paper.

- A BONE FOLDER, a small tool that looks kind of like a tongue depressor. It is used for making well-defined creases, such as the fold in a card. You probably have an adequate substitute — a utensil with a round handle, a Popsicle stick, even a fingernail.

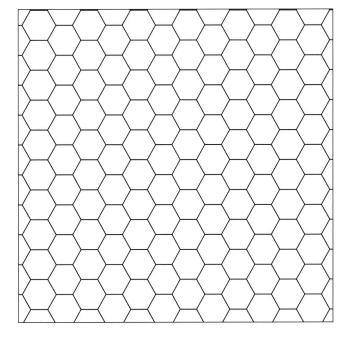

This hex-design grid is made up of hex units. Feel free to copy it, change the scale, or modify it in a way that suits you.

- PICTURES. If you are designing an identifiable figure, have a few pictures to which you can refer.
- Two pieces of HEAVY CARDBOARD OR BOOK BOARD. The example used book board, cut to 4-1/2" square.
- FIVE SQUARES OF LIGHT-COLORED CARD STOCK, 8-3/4" square. These will become the pages of the journal.
- TWO LENGTHS OF STRONG RIBBON, 24" long. The ribbon will be used to keep the journal closed when you are not using it.
- HEX GRAPH PAPER (provided on previous page)

Weaving the Figure

Remember that with hex weave the figure is created by the outline of the units and will be drawn by the strips. This project is more open than the ones before, so you can either work through the example with me or you can design your own figure and take these steps as suggestions.

Note: A lot of my work is garden-inspired, and I will be designing a butterfly that I can use as an embellishment.

○ STEP ONE: Sketch out a preliminary figure, using your hex grid or graph paper.

○ STEP TWO: Step back and look at the overall design — Is it what you want? More importantly, is it the right scale? In a few chapters, we will consider scale in some detail, but for now, assume that the distance between successive hex units in the same direction is a little more three times the width of the strips. We have generally been using one-quarter inch strips, so each hex unit is between three quarters of an inch and an inch wide.

Don't be taken in by the small size of the first butterfly image; the image has been substantially reduced. The picture is to show the design, which is far too large — more than seven inches!

This solution is an interesting image, though. I made the first wing and then mirrored and copied the first to make a symmetrical set of wings. This would be fun to experiment with, but right now we have to distill the essential visual characteristics of a butterfly.

There are at least a half-dozen variations of this simple little figure. It can have or not have wing tips. Try experimenting with different edgings. You can add a butterfly body by pasting in a rectangle. If you try to fold the butterfly gently, it will fold easily at a point not quite at the middle. Repeat the fold on the other side and you will get a small rectangle that you can use to balance the butterfly in an upright position.

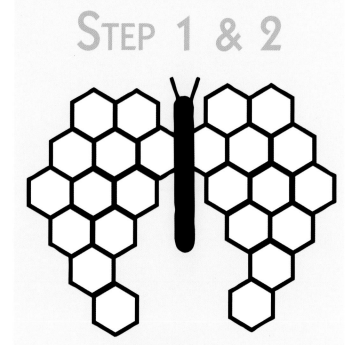

STEP 1 & 2

My first butterfly design – too big!

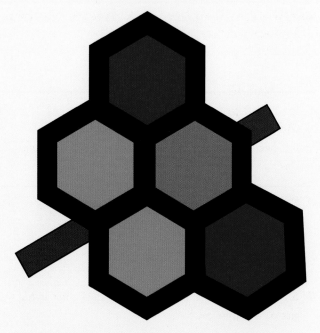

Small butterfly, approximately 3" x 3". *Essence of Butterfly* proved to look less like a butterfly than the first, but it is evocative of the small winged creatures that frequent my summer garden.

A flutter of butterflies. Constructed using 1/4" strips, approximately 3" x 3" each. This little group of butterflies shows some of the variations possible in even a small figure.

If you are not happy with your figure, repeat steps one and two until you create a figure that is pleasing to you.

○ STEP THREE: Weave a multi-hex "sheet" that is big enough to contain your design. Don't forget to add enough extra units for any edgings you plan to use.

○ STEP FOUR: Turn your hex sheet over, and glue the woven strips together by painting a very light coat of glue over the whole back. (Glue will seep through to the front of the sheet, so lay the sheet on something that will not stick to your design, like wax paper.)

○ STEP FIVE: Once the glue has dried, draw your cutting lines, and cut out your figure from the back, following the cutting line exactly. It is very easy to go off on the wrong path and cut something that is important to the design.

○ STEP SIX: Cut out the figure and immediately put a little white glue all along the cut edges.

○ STEP SEVEN: Add an edging if desired.

○ STEP EIGHT: Varnish the figure.

Choose the Backing

Pick out a backing for the completed figure that makes it sparkle. Try putting the figure on a variety of backgrounds and see which ones make the figure pop!

Make Covers

This time we will glue on the hex figure as the last step. It protects the figure from abrasion during construction and if you make an early mistake in the cover, you haven't also lost your figure.

○ STEP ONE: Make certain that your board has been cut large enough to contain your entire figure.

○ STEP TWO: Cut a square of decorative paper about an 1-1/2" longer and wider than the cover. Turn it over with the wrong side up. Center the cardboard on the paper, face down, and glue them together.

○ STEP THREE: You have to trim the corners of the background paper so that you don't have big lumps where you have excess paper. Mark your cutting lines before you cut. Cut the corners of the backing paper at each point of the board, leaving enough paper to equal twice the thickness of the board.

() STEP FOUR: Using your bone folder, carefully smooth the remaining paper up the sides of the board, then fold it over the back of the board, making a cover that is mitered, or looks somewhat like "hospital corners." Glue the wings of the paper to the back of the board.

The journal cover shows several stages of construction. You can see how close the edge of the paper is to the point of the board, the width of the sides that will be folded over to the back, and the first folded corner.

The inside of the finished cover. The accordion will be glued to the white square.

You now have a board that is almost completely covered by the paper, except for a piece in the center of the back. Not to worry. Cut a piece of paper — your choice — into a square that completely covers the hole and glue it on. Later, the accordion body will be glued to the covers just at that point.

You have just completed one of the covers of the journal. You will need two of these, so make a second. You will be surprised at how much easier the second one is than the first!

The front of the finished cover.

STEP FIVE: Now, we make the accordion. You will want your covers to extend a little beyond the pages to protect them, say an eighth of an inch all around. Measure your covers, and cut a square of the heavy, smooth, light-color paper to use as pages. The size of the pages depends on the size of the covers (although with very special paper it might work the other way around). The rule determining the size of the paper is this: subtract two times the width of the desired margin from the top and the side of the square. In practice, we will usually want one-eighth inch margins, so cut the paper to be a square one-quarter inch shorter than twice the cover. In this example, the side of the paper to cut is $(2 \times 4.5") - (2 \times 0.125") = 8.75"$. Cut five of these squares.

Making the Accordion

We have to make three folds in order to create the accordion page.

STEP 1: The first fold is diagonal. Make only one diagonal fold. Do **not** make the corresponding diagonal fold on the other side.

STEP 2: Turn the paper over. Make the second and third folds, which are horizontal and vertical, and are both folded on the side opposite from which the diagonal was folded.

STEP 5

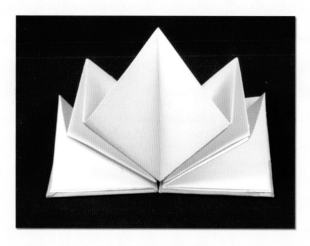

Another view of the accordion, with pages opening.

Open the folded paper, and turn it so that the front side is facing up. You can see from the diagram that the original square has now been divided into four small squares, two of which have a fold across their diagonal and two that have not been folded.

STEP 1　　STEP 2

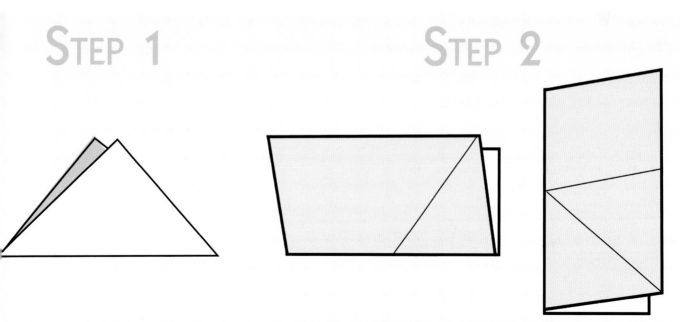

The first diagonal fold. The white side is the outside.

The first straight fold. The diagonal fold is shown as the lighter line.

The third fold. Both the straight and diagonal folds are shown.

◯ STEP 3: Pick up the paper, and gently push down on the center of the diagonal ridge. It will fold itself into quarters. The small squares that were not folded become the top and bottom squares, and the previously folded squares on the inside provide the ability to open and close. Fold all five pages.

Assembling the Accordion

◯ STEP 1: Take two of the five original papers, now folded, and hold one in your left hand so that the inside is facing up, and hold the other in your right hand so that the inside is facing down. Slide the topmost leaf of the one in your right hand over the bottommost leaf of the one in your left, until the top and bottom interweave and the two sets of pages are joined. If your cutting and folding are accurate, the two pieces will overlap almost completely. They do have to be glued, however. The same process is repeated with the next two pieces. You can add pages on either end of the accordion as long you always merge an upside down piece with a right-side-up piece.

◯ STEP 2: Adding the last large square takes some thinking. In order for your books to open fully and gracefully, remember two things: first, you have to begin with an odd number of large squares so that the two ends of the accordion are mirror images — weavers and knitters do the same thing when they add some extra threads or stitches "to balance"; second, it works better to begin and end the accordion with an "up-facing" unit. When you open an up-facing journal, the pages curl towards you and invite you to come inside. Down-facing journals tend to curl away from you and are harder to manage.

◯ STEP 3: You will want to have some way of keeping your book closed when you are not using it. The simplest one is to glue a ribbon to the inside of the cover before gluing the accordion to the cover. Center the ribbon over the center of the cover,

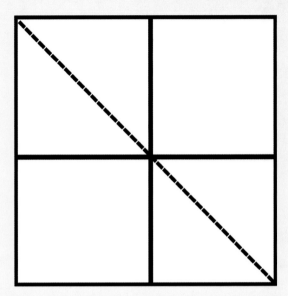

The paper folds for the accordion book pages.

so you have equally long loose ends, about ten inches. Repeat with the other cover. Now you have four lengths of ribbon you can use tie the covers together at the sides.

◯ STEP 4: All that remains is to glue the ends of the accordion to the covers and to glue your hex figure to the front of the book. For both the accordion and the hex figure, apply glue to the back of the piece that is being placed. The item that is being placed is generally smaller, and you don't want extra glue extending beyond the smaller figure. It also gives you more time to position the piece being glued. Glue the ends of your accordion to the covers and then glue the back of your hex figure and attach it to the cover.

Congratulations!

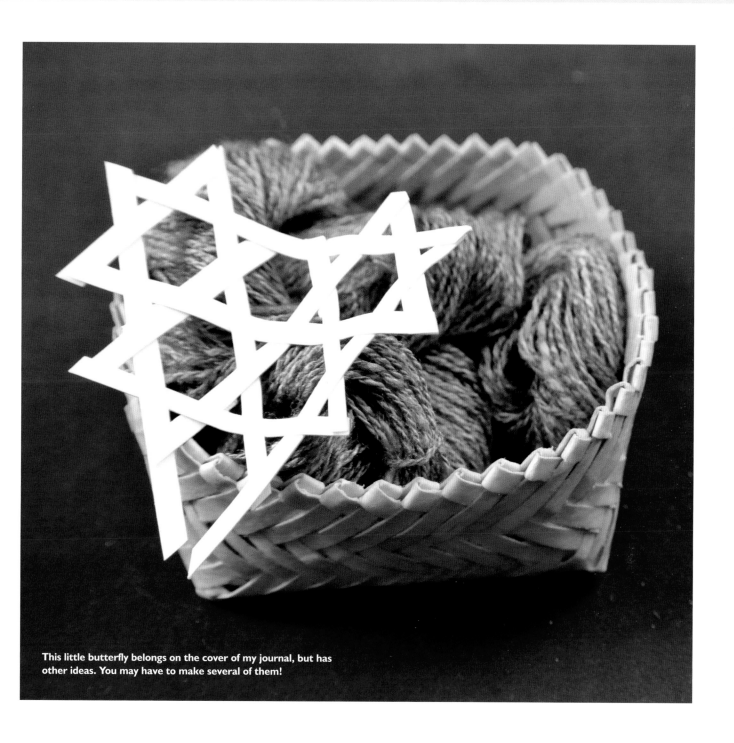

This little butterfly belongs on the cover of my journal, but has other ideas. You may have to make several of them!

So far, we have been looking at patterns that can be made by constructing and manipulating hex units. Now, let us move down a level and begin to look at the patterns we can obtain by varying the colors of individual strips. Most of the rest of this book focuses on the effects of combining weave structure with color variations.

We began by learning how to create hex units, and then how to design with them, but we have just begun to explore this versatile weave structure. In this chapter, we will focus on color. The next chapter is a quick consideration of scale. The remaining chapters introduce mad weave, which explodes with color and pattern.

COLOR AND TRIAXIAL PATTERNS

Think of color as a combination of HUE, VALUE, and SATURATION.

- HUE refers to the color names we generally use to describe a color ("blue," "red," "green.") We also use the terms "cool" colors — the purple, blue, and green side of the spectrum — and "warm" colors" — the yellow, orange, red side of the spectrum. Warm colors appear to move towards you and are more energizing. Cool colors seem to move away and are more calming. Americans have an enduring preference for blue.

- VALUE is the brightness of a color along a scale from white to black. It is measured in percentages, with black at zero and white at one-hundred. Artists often use a ten-point scale with white at the top and black on the bottom, and we will use it here.

- SATURATION is the dominance of hue in the color. Saturation is also measured in percentages, with the pure color at one-hundred percent. The range of saturation is from a pure color to the gray corresponding to the value of the color. For example, if the brightness of the value is one-hundred percent, the range of saturation will be from the pure hue to white.

Triaxial weaving enables us to explore the interactions of color among three directions at once, as compared to the two directions of biaxial weaving. Value becomes the critical component. If the values between the strips are not equal steps apart, the two closest values "group" together and are perceived as a single value.

In hex weave, in particular, there is some space between adjacent intersections, so it is likely that there are some subtle differences in apparent color within the same strip, depending on whether it is in an intersection or by itself against a background.

Below are some generalizations we have made from our experiences with triaxial weaving. In making these observations, we have assumed that the size of the projects is small — small enough that it can all be seen at one glance. If you have to move your head to see the whole composition, you will lose some of the color effects. Remember, also, that our visual fields are about twice as wide as they are high, so that a horizontal image is more easily scanned than a vertical image. For hex weaves of three or more colors, we find:

- When you want to emphasize the hexagonal structure of the weave, pick colors that are relatively similar in value, no more than two steps apart; for example, values 2, 4, and 5. When you want to emphasize the individual colors of the strips, increase the steps in value between the colors in the set.

- Hue also plays a part in color melding. It is easier for two colors to blend if they are close together in the color wheel. If you want to encourage color blending, pick colors of related hue and value.

- If you use three (or more) colors of about the same value, you will probably find that one will stand out as being a little different and will dominate. This can be maddening, but it is also instructive.

To illustrate these effects, compare the two drawings below. The first has three colors that are similar in value. It is a low-energy, calming image, and your eye has no trouble tracing the outlines of the figure or the hexagonal spaces. In contrast, the second drawing is lively and disconnected. Even though the three colors are the same hues, they have been changed in brightness and saturation. Our eyes have a hard time focusing on one point or moving in an orderly way around the figure when the individual groups of color demand to be seen. Which to choose? It depends on what you are doing with the piece. If you want the observer to be relaxed, choose values that are close, cool, and, perhaps, a little boring. If you want to engage the viewer, and perhaps make the viewer a little edgy, emphasize differences in brightness and saturation.

 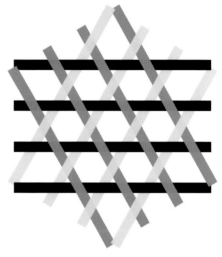

Values of these three sets of strips are almost the same.   Values of these three sets of strips are very different.

Color Placement

Color placement is one of the chief factors that directs where we look when we first see an object. Generally, our eyes are drawn to areas of high contrast, so a scattering of light elements can induce quite a lot of movement.

The amount and direction of movement across a figure is also related to the way the colors are presented. Look at the two drawings — each were made using the same colored strips. The first one has the darkest color in the middle of the figure and the lightest color on the edge. Overall, this arrangement has some depth as we are drawn into the center. In contrast, the second drawing has the lightest color in the middle and the darkest color on the edge. The tendency for the lightest color to appear to move closer to the viewer means that the center of the image moves forward and the image becomes flatter.

The values run darkest in the center to lightest at   The values are lightest in the center and darkest at
the edge.   the edge.

Multi-color Interactions

This clock illustrates what can happen when you vary everything at once! The hex weave combines two colors that are low in saturation with a third color that is of medium saturation. The lightest is pale green with an overall diamond pattern and a few tiny spots of sparkle. The next set of strips is a light pearlized taupe. The medium-saturation strips are peach and brown. The background is a slightly lighter color-way of the taupe strips, and the border is a slightly brighter peach than in the medium strips. There is a peachy-brown vintage button at the top to indicate twelve o'clock.

When the hex weave was completed and assembled, a number of transformations occurred. The peach-colored border energized the peach in the medium-value strips, which then popped up and became the dominant set of strips. The two lighter strips looked much more different when they were just separate uncut sheets of paper. The taupe strips usually melt into the background and take the green strips with them. In some lights, the clock appears to have only the medium-value strips. In other lights and angles, the green strips appear and compete with the darker strips for dominance. Changing the background color or the border made significant differences in the way that the strips were perceived.

Most of the effects were as anticipated, but the overall image, which changes with the lighting, border, and background, is more complex and most charming.

The clock, *Cinderella Comes to the Ball*, shows multiple interactions between the strips, the background, and the lighting.

Gradients

Gradients are wonderful additions to a hex weave. They provide a lovely, graceful movement of color across the face of the fabric.

Each of the three directions in this small hoop has a different gradient. What keeps order amidst all the changes is that they are all within a narrow set of values and saturation.

The thin strips are not part of the weave structure, and could be removed without altering the hex weave generated by the wider strips. The thin strips are an embellishment. The wide holes of the hex weave demand to be filled. In Chapter Six, we will fill the holes with additional strips and call it "Mad Weave"!

This small hanging was woven using hand-dyed, heavy watercolor paper on an embroidery hoop. Size, 6" in diameter.

✳IN SEARCH OF THE BULL'S EYE

A bull's eye pattern is composed of concentric circles of color, like a dart board. It would seem that hex weave would shine at circular weaving, but it turns out to be a little tricky. There are three likely ways of producing circles.

1. The solution that most people try first (including the authors) is to use strips that are two colors: one color at the top half and one at the bottom half.

The scheme does not work. Each strip has two ends and the ends are different colors. Since two colors fanned out together cannot make a single-colored bull's eye, this solution is not possible. The schematic drawing of three strips shows the problem.

The experiment was not a total loss, however. Notice that by grouping colors together, you can easily mass colors.

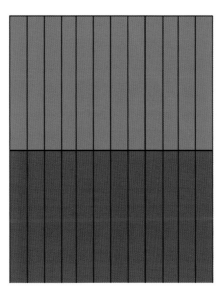

The paper before cutting. Each strip will be half red and half green.

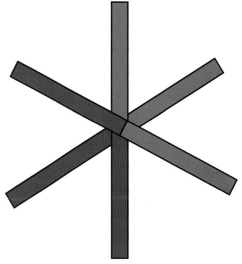

The schematic drawing shows why half-and-half strips cannot make a bull's eye. This restriction is not limited to triaxial weaving, but holds for any circular form that uses two-color strips.

2. Next possibility: If all the legs must be the same color, let us just try to add the second color in the middle. Call it the center-stripe pattern.

This solution doesn't work either, but it shows some potential. The center color is solid for the first several rows, but then the base color begins to take over. With each new row, the hex weave gets a little wider, but the center color stays the same width. Eventually, the base color dominates almost completely, but there will always be six streaks of the stripe color.

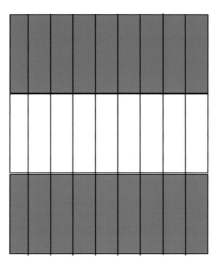

This is the paper set-up for the center-stripe pattern.

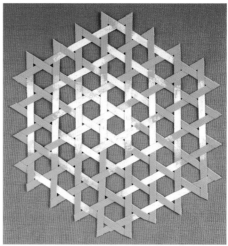

The photograph of this second attempt looks like a white spiderweb in a tree.

3. This solution takes the second possibility a step farther. We can eliminate the tails of the center by never having them. We can paint only a dozen strips with the center-stripe pattern, which will give us a solid center, and then grow the hexagon using strips the same color as the legs of the strips that carried the central stripe.

So, we can build a single-circle Bull's Eye, but we have only postponed the problem. As soon as we add a third color, we are in the legs problem again. Once you have added a strip, its leg will extend to the outer edge of the piece. The color of the new strips will interact with the color of the existing strips, and we no longer have a single-color circle. It doesn't work.

Fortunately, while in pursuit of the elusive bull's eye, we came up with some interesting effects to explore further. It's the things we take for granted that trip us!

QUICK START PROJECT

▨ FAUX BULL'S EYE CLOCK

Whether or not it is a true bull's eye, you will often see designs in which there is a center figure with concentric rings around it. Let's do one together.

This project has a center bull's eye and two colors to make two concentric hexagons around the central hex figure. The background adds a fourth color. We want the direction of movement to be out of the center. What have we learned about color? We know that lighter colors seem to push out towards you and dark colors draw back. We want, then, to put the lightest color on the very edge of the weaving, so that we can keep the light color from distracting our eyes in some other color's row. The dark value should be in the center, where its tendency to pull back makes its long legs less obtrusive. The remaining hex color needs to be about in the middle of the darkest and lightest strips. The background should also be an intermediate value, and preferably not of the same family as any of the strips.

This clock was made from heavy scrap-booking paper, and measures about twelve inches by twelve inches

Supplies

- A CLOCK BODY AND HANDS. You can purchase the clock parts at many craft stores. There are many Internet companies that sell clock parts as well. Check the "Resources" section at the end of the book for several Internet sites. Small, accurate, quartz clocks and hands will probably cost less than ten dollars.
- HEAVY CARDBOARD, such as poster board or book-binder board. You will mount your clock face and decorative backing on the board for strength and stability.
- A DRILL. The drill only has to make a 3/8" hole, drilling through the paper affixed to a heavy cardboard backing.

Weaving the Design

◯ STEP ONE: Make a single hex unit (six strips) with your darkest color. Follow with one row (six strips) of the medium color and then six strips of the lightest color. You now have what looks like a center hexagon with two concentric rows of different colors.

◯ STEP TWO: Add whatever edging you were planning; glue the edges. Now, glue the completed figure to a decorative background, and then glue the whole piece to the board.

◯ STEP THREE: Find the center of your piece. (Remember that you have to find the center in three directions.) Drill a hole 3/8" through the center.

◯ STEP FOUR: Insert the clock body, following the simple (really!) instructions that come with the clock.

◯ STEP FIVE: Frame the clock, if desired — and hang it up!

▣ THE FRAMER AND THE FRAMED

Hex weave can serve as a frame for images that are visible through the open hexagonal spaces of the hex units or it can itself be the focus of a piece.

In Haunted, a dark blue hex screen was dropped over a confusing mad weave pattern. The clear boundaries of the hex weave organized the underlying picture so that it seems to be a series of windows that we can look through. The focus is on the background and not on the hex frame.

In contrast, Fragment consists only of layers of hex weave. I stacked three pieces of hex weave on top of each other to create depth, and also augmented the feeling of depth by placing the layers with the darker and duller colors in the lower layers. The background in this piece is typically not noticed.

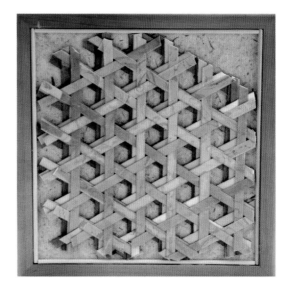

Fragment was inspired by an archeological expedition.
Size: 6" x 6".

Haunted has a mad weave base and a hex weave cover. Size: 6" x 6".

Other than for the button, *Spaceship Landing* is entirely composed of individual hex units. Approximately 5" x 5".

In *Adam and Eve in a Field of Apples*, hex weaves combine nicely with mad weave, even if the pieces are at a different scale.

Individual hex units can be combined in numerous ways, similar to modular origami. In Spaceship Landing, a vintage button sits on top of three individual, sparkling white stars that are graduated in size. The stars themselves rest on a nest of fourteen individual hex units that have been interlocked and gently curved.

It is surprisingly easy to play with the individual hexes and devise interesting patterns that can be curved around so that you get a circle in which the first and last elements connect at the finish. The resulting figure looks like a wreath.

In Adam and Eve in a Field of Apples, two individual hex units are intertwined to make an enhancement for an underlying mad weave.

ENHANCEMENTS TO HEX WEAVES

The open spaces in hex weaves call out to be filled. Usually, the space is filled by more strips or an underlying image, but you don't have to stop there. You can add beads, buttons, text, ribbons — almost anything that can tolerate being woven. You can weave plain weave or any weave structure that is compatible with the underlying hex weave.

Conversely, you can make hex weave be the embellishment for other base fabrics, such as knitting or weaving. Details for doing this are a more advanced topic, but briefly, you make strips out of fabric or use ribbon or yarn and attach a set of parallel strips to the background. The parallel strips become the strips of one of the directions of the hex weave, and you can weave the strips of the other two directions on the tied-down strips.

I recently met Tim Roth, an artist who combines pottery with a wide variety of caning patterns. His work is beautiful, and it sent me scurrying back to my basketry books. Although a majority of patterns are octagonal, there are some great hexagonal patterns.

The three photos below are my first three cane-inspired designs. The designs are practically identical — they each begin with a compound hex with six strips per side, for a total of eighteen strips. The hex weave is the base and is woven first, and then the bases are embellished with a second design that is woven directly onto the first. The embellishment requires fifteen strips of a second color: five strips per direction, so that the finished figure has alternating colors and a hex weave strip at each end.

There are countless ways to incorporate caning patterns into hex weave, which of course is one of the earliest basketry patterns itself. It is beyond the scope of this book to explore caning patterns as they apply to triaxial weaving, but, at this point, it's a good challenge for you to develop your own basketry-embellished hex weaves. Have fun — and when you find patterns you like, save them!

Pennsylvania sunsets can be dramatic, and the red and purple ones are the best! The treasure box uses two colors of medium value that are also next to each other on the color wheel. In addition, each is made of patterned scrapbooking paper and has some patterning of the color of the other within it. We might predict that these factors would over-ride the pattern, but the differences in value, the frequent repetition of the pattern, and the strong diagonal lines make the pattern visible.

This small treasure box, *Seven Seas*, looks like a very old map. 4.25" x 4.25". A yellow-green strip was used as a base and then was paired with its complement — a red/purple hue that was lightened so that it was lighter than the green.

Caning-pattern embellishment. Size: clock, 10.5" x 10.5"; Hex weave, 5" x 6". The most dramatic example has the greatest difference in the values of the base and the embellishment. The base is a sparkling eggplant color and the embellishment color is pale yellow, for large differences in value. In addition, the colors are on opposite sides of the color wheel, creating a large difference in hue. These factors work together to produce a bold graphic.

Now that you have some experience with constructing hex weave, you have probably found that the figures are surprisingly large. Chapter Seven shows how to change a hex weave into a hex-derived mad weave, which is much denser, but for now let's keep our focus on hex weave.

You control the size of the hex weave by the width of the strips you use. Each hex unit will be a little more than three times the width of the strip. This is almost true. In reality, the flexibility of the strips has an effect on the tightness of the weave, and most of the time, you also have to add one extra strip width to balance the design. You should probably allow closer to three and a half times the width of the hex units, but you will have to experiment to get the exact numbers for your strips and how tightly you weave.

If you are not geometrically inclined, you can skip the rest of this section. Just remember two important facts: You control the size of your weaving by how wide you make the strips, and each hex unit will be a little more than three times the width of the strips.

If you thoroughly liked geometry, read on.

CALCULATIONS

Determining the Area of a Hexagon

Suppose you have a project that has to fit a particular size and you need to compute the size of your design. Remember that a regular hexagon can be divided into six identical equilateral triangles. The formula for the area of one equilateral triangle is: Area = 1/2 (base x height).

We know the length of the base — we have either assigned it or we can measure it directly. We can also find the height if we know the length of the base. Drop a plumb line from the top of the triangle to the base. Because this is an equilateral triangle, we have bisected the base and created two identical right triangles, back-to-back.

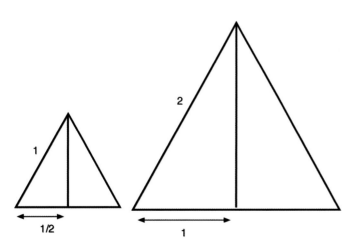

Just to make this a little clearer, imagine that we have two equilateral triangles. The first has legs that are one inch long. The second has two-inch legs. How do they compare in size and area?

The other formula we need to do this calculation is the Pythagorean Theorem: The square of the length of the hypotenuse is equal to the sum of the squares of the two adjacent sides.

$$c^2 = a^2 + b^2:$$
"c" is the hypotenuse, "a"
is the base, and "b" is the height

The large triangle has legs twice as long as the small one.

We know two of the values, so we can solve for the third. The 1" triangle has a 1" hypotenuse and the bisected base is now half of its original length, or 1/2". Solving the equation to get the height, we use this version of the Pythagorean Theorem:

$$c2 - a2 = b2$$
$$1 - (1/2)2 = b2$$
$$b = .866" = \text{the height of the triangle}$$

Now that we have the height of the equilateral triangle, we can solve for the area.

$$\text{Area} = 1/2 \text{ (base x height)}$$
$$\text{Area} = 1/2 \text{ (1" x .867")} = .433 \text{ square inches}$$

There are six equilateral triangles in a hexagon, so the area of the hexagon is 6 x .433 or 2.598 square inches. For the two-inch triangle, we know that the hypotenuse is 2" and the bisected base is 1", so the height is:

$$c2 - a2 -= b2$$
$$(4-1) = b$$
$$b = 1.732 \text{ inches}$$

The area of the equilateral triangle is 1/2 (2)(1.732) = 1.732 square inches, and the area of the 2" hexagon = 6 x 1.732 or 10.392 square inches.

Divide 10.392 by 2.598 and, allowing for some rounding error, the answer is 4. This number tells us that if we double the length of a side of a hexagon, the area of the hexagon will be four times as large.

While we were looking for the relative areas, we also solved another question: If we look at the width of an equilateral triangle from side-to-side and compare that value to the width of the triangle from point-to-point, we find that the side-to-side width is 86.6 % of the width when measured point-to-point. That means that if a hexagon is sitting on its base, it is 86.6% of its height when it is balancing on a point.

Why are we interested in this? Suppose you are doing a commission and you had ten inches to work with and the customer loved a fifteen-hex design. How big can you make the hexes? We have been working with 1/4" strips, but each hex unit is then almost one inch. Fifteen hexes at close to one inch in width apiece is clearly too wide. Divide ten inches by fifteen units, and the answer is that for each hex unit, you need to reduce the width of the hex figure itself to 67% of its current size. If we assume that the hex unit is three times the width of the strip, we multiply 1/4" by .67 and find out that the new strips should be .17 inches, or about three-sixteenth of an inch. (Even though three-sixteenth, at 0.1875, is a little larger than .17, we allowed for some wiggle room since four of the one-quarter inch strips did not quite total an inch. Three-sixteens is much easier to measure!)

THE EFFECTS OF SCALE

When we double the length and width of a strip, we see a figure that is four times as large. The increase in size of the strip changes the ways we look at it. Thin strips can be unobtrusive, quietly framing whatever is in the central hexagonal space, but heavy strips cannot be denied.

For example, let us look more carefully at the mobiles that were examples from your second project on Page 14. The strips of the paper trees were all the same width. The differences in size among the various tree layers was due to the differences in the edgings.

In contrast, each of the stars in the three-star mobile made from wood veneer uses exactly the same pattern. There is no difference in edgings. The differences in scale between the stars is the width of the strip. The strips for weaving the stars were made of a complicated veneer. The largest star was made from using the full width of the veneer. I then peeled off small pieces of the veneer to make the strips narrower so that each star would be a little smaller than the one before it. What I was not expecting was that the large star doesn't only look larger, it looks different from the smaller stars, bolder and more commanding.

This chapter concludes the introduction to radial hex weave. The next chapter presents layered hex weave — another way of weaving hex that makes it easy to progress to mad weave.

In the earlier chapters, we worked with radial hex weave, where we began at the center of the hex weave and worked our way around and around the hexagon until we reached the outside edge. Now, we are going to show you hex weave in a way you have probably not seen, even if you are familiar with hex weave. Try this version! It is simple and fast, and leads directly into mad weave.

QUICK START PROJECT

❋LAYERED HEX COLOR GAMP

We are going to weave a gamp, a way of creating a warp in which each color can woven with itself and every other color in the same piece.

Supplies

- SCISSORS
- HEAVY PAPER (or other flexible strips, such as quilting fabric or ribbons)
- GLUE
- TAPE

Weaving the Gamp

○ STEP 1: Choose six strip colors (patterned papers are okay). Include one color that you love, one color you dislike, and four colors that range from neutral to positive, and cut three sets of strips for a total of eighteen strips. Now, lay out one of the sets of six colors in some order that makes sense to you.

○ STEP 2: Cut the paper into strips: 1-4" x 12"

○ STEP 3: Lay out tape, sticky side up.

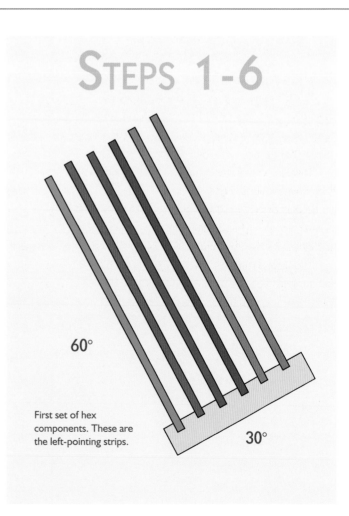

STEPS 1-6

60°

30°

First set of hex components. These are the left-pointing strips.

- ○ STEP 4: Plan out your strip sequence. Lay the strips on the tape, using only half the width of the tape. Leave large spaces between strips, a little more than twice the width of the strips.

- ○ STEP 5: Fold over the tape so that the strips are anchored front and back.

- ○ STEP 6: Pin the package to your work surface at a 60° angle, with the taped ends facing you.

- ○ STEP 7: Make a second set of strips with the strips in reverse order.

- ○ STEP 8: Place the second set of strips on top of the first, so that there is a 60° angle between the two sets.

- ○ STEP 9: Begin by lashing the two components together using the third set of strips. The weaving is more stable when you have the taped end close to you, so turn the work surface so that the loose ends are facing away from you.

- ○ STEP 10: Take the green strip from the third set of strips and weave it through the two green strips and also the purple strips next to them.

First two sets of hex components: left- and right-pointing strips.

It is the mandate of the third set to bring all the strips of the first and second sets into a single plane, so the third set of strips will always travel over the upper layer, pushing it down, and under the lower layer, pulling it up. The path of that first green strip becomes "under the purple strip to bring it up, over the green strip to push it down, under the second (left-pointing) green to bring it up, and over the second purple strip to push it down." The upper and lower levels never intersect with each other. They only intersect with the third layer.

There are several interesting things happening here. We continue to maintain the "over-under-over-under" plain weave structure by alternating strips from the upper and lower levels. Once you lay down the second set of strips on top of or underneath the first set, you have created a left-handed or right-handed figure committed to weaving with a specific set of rules. Each member of the three components retains its group membership: All right-pointing strips point right. They never point left. A right-pointing strip never becomes a left-pointing strip or a horizontal strip either. It's the Plain Weave Rule again: A strip can do almost anything as long as it doesn't affect the tabby structure of the weave.

The second strip to weave is purple, then blue, red, khaki, and taupe. Just follow the line of same-color crosses. When you have finished the last strip, you will have a big triangle, but you'll also have more unwoven ends that you can weave — repeat the pattern to see what happens at the transition, reverse the pattern, or introduce new colors. There are many variations, so explore!

This is a hex-weave color gamp, where you can see many three-strip interactions of eight different colors. The paper used was scrap-booking paper, one-quarter inch wide and twelve inches long, with elongated hexagons. The gamp is approximately nine-and-one-half inches by eleven inches.

We have looked at two different ways of weaving hex weave: the radial and layered approaches. The most obvious difference is that the radial method is more suited to projects that are circular, and the layered method is more linear. With the layered method, you also can see the skeleton of the whole project as you are adding strips, an advantage if you are designing as you go. I believe that the radial system is faster, although we have yet to stage the hex-weave Olympics!

This concludes our study of hex weave as a stand-alone weave structure, although we will encounter it again in the next chapter, Chapter Seven, as we develop hex-based mad weave. In Chapter Eight, we will present a second way of weaving — mad weave — that will eventually take us back to the loom.

In the first six chapters, we have looked at individual hex weaves in some detail. Now we are going to combine hex weaves to make mad weave.

Mad weave is the second simplest triaxial weave. For weavers, mad weave is the juxtaposition of a 2/1 twill and a 1/2 twill, woven using three axes instead of two. For those not familiar with weaving terminology, think of the woven fabric of your blue jeans. Mad weave always has three layers at any given point and is a solid construction, so it is sturdy and uses a surprising amount of material. It also doesn't drape very well, but it lies flat and hangs straight. Household furnishings, such as runners, pillows, window shades, place-mats, and quilts, are ideal, and so are some articles of clothing that are straight, such as some vests, tabards, and scarves (see photo).

Remember that all of the patterning in hex and mad weave is due to the way you use the colors of the strips with which you build. There are no structural differences between designs. You only have to learn one construction to be able to construct any other pattern!

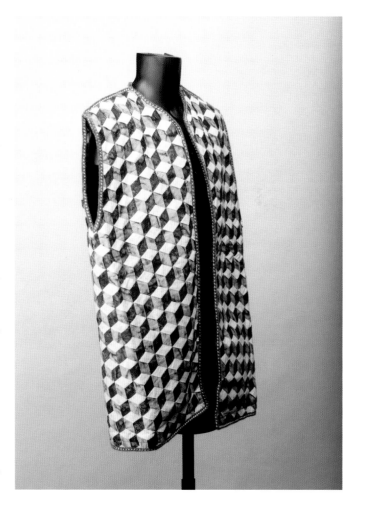

Contemporary vest, c. 2008.
Photography by Bruce Waters. Courtesy of the weaver, Luciano Abbarno.

QUICK START PROJECT

❈HEX-BASED MAD WEAVE

Now that you are fairly conversant with hex weave, let's look at the relationship between hex weave and hex-based mad weave. Hex-based mad weave is constructed by placing one hex weave on top of a second hex weave and then lashing them together with the as-yet-unwoven strips of a third hex weave. Think of mad weave as a quilt — there is a top layer, a bottom layer, and an element that connects the two other layers.

Before we look carefully at specific patterns, we will build a hex-based mad weave that will be a great reference when you need a refresher, so pull out your simplest strips in three colors. You don't need any supplies that you don't already have.

However, you will need a lot of strips: twelve strips of each color. Mad weave takes three times as many strips as does a hex weave of the same size. In essence, we are filling in those tantalizing holes in the center of the hex units.

() STEP 1: Make two small hex weaves. Using one color per hex weave, weave two individual 3 x 3 x 3 hexes (see Chapter Three). Make sure that both are either right-handed or left-handed — or you will have difficulty integrating them.

() STEP 2: Position layers. Place one of the two hexes on top of the other to check that they are about the same size and shape. Don't worry if there are some minor differences, but if they are very different, tighten them up and try again. If you have trouble with your angles, try using one of the angle tools in the appendix.

() STEP 3: Once the two weaves are well aligned, move the top layer down one-half of a hex unit and also one-half of a hex unit to the right. You can see the triangles of the bottom layer framed by the holes in the top layer, and you can see the triangles of the top layer hovering over the spaces of the bottom. If you are using ribbon or something silky and slippery, pin the ends of your strips to your work surface.

Mark several of the framed triangles so that you don't lose your bearing. It is easy to forget which strips are the framed triangles, especially if they are not all the same color. Take a piece of string and weave it in and out off several of the framed triangles. You will remove it later.

() STEP 4: The first lasher, the horizontal component of the lashing layer. The dark strip shows the path of the first lasher; the lower hex weave level is blue, the upper level is pink. The job of the lashing strips is to raise the lower strips and constrain the upper set. There is no direct interaction between the red and blue strips — the lasher does all the work.

The first set of lashers is easy. It is simply "over two strips, under two strips." Where do we begin this pattern? Begin with any triangle from the lower level — in this case, a blue triangle. The lashers will always dive under the triangle as they do their job in bringing the lower layer up to the plane of the upper level, and then will emerge on the other side of the triangle in order to travel over the next two strips, which are from the top layer. The lashers will not cover the lower-level triangles.

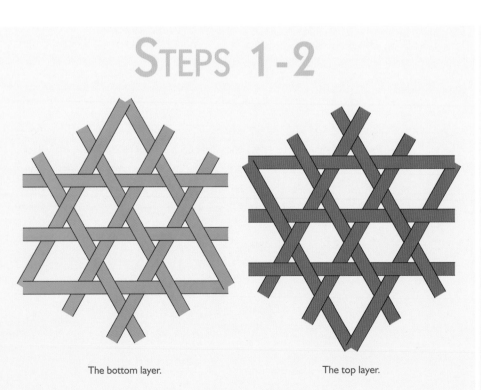

STEPS 1-2

The bottom layer.

The top layer.

STEP 3

Two hex weaves ready to be lashed.

STEP 4

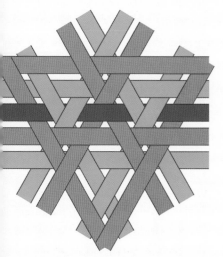

Close-up of the path of the first set of lashing strips. The dark strip shows the path of the first group of lashers.

STEP 5

Completed horizontal lashers.

STEP 6

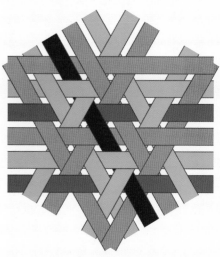

The path of the second set of lashers. The dark blue strip shows the new pathway.

◯ STEP 5: You can pick any one direction to begin, but complete the lashing in that direction before moving on to the next. ("Any direction" means any one component — for example, all the horizontal strips of layer three, or all the left-pointing strips of layer three.) These strips will all be parallel.

◯ STEP 6: Begin the second set of lashers.

The second lashing pattern has changed. Let's take a brief back-step and look at the bottom-level triangles peeking through the holes in the upper layer in Step Three. You will see that each lower-level triangle has three slots, one along each side. These slots are the places where the lasher dives under the triangle and up the other side. Also note that lashers cannot go directly across the triangle to reach a second slot, but have to go to one or the other of the adjacent slots. The second lasher path still goes under the lower-level triangles, but it also travels over one of its own layer of lashers. Instead of a pattern that says "under the lower-level triangle, over two strips," the new pattern is "under the lower-level triangle, and over all of the strips until the next lower-level triangle.

How do I know whether I have added the lashers correctly? We go back to the basic triangle.

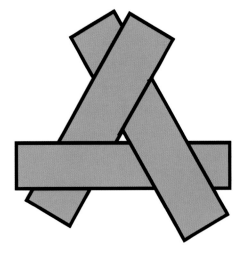

Basic right-hand triangle. Note that every intersection resolves to a right-pointing element.

Whenever any two strips intersect, the one that is on top determines the handedness, so the placement of the first two strips of the bottom layer will set the paths for the whole piece. The critical issue is to keep placing the lashers so that they preserve the handedness of the project.

Basic right-hand triangle with first lasher.

The second lasher also goes under the triangle, but, first, it has to go over the initial lasher to preserve the right-handedness of the mad weave. Look at the crossing of the two yellow strips: the top strip is pointing right. If we had crossed the strips so that the first lasher was on top, we would have introduced a left-handed element into a right-handed mad weave. For example, look at the configuration labeled "incorrect" to see a left-handed error (below center). Compare the correct drawing with this one (below right). In general, this mixed pairing will not work and you will lose your pattern. The path of the second set of lashers is "over the horizontal lasher, under the triangle, using the bottom/left-side slot."

Now we can finish our hex-based mad weave.

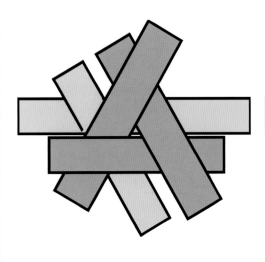

Basic right-hand triangle with two lashers.

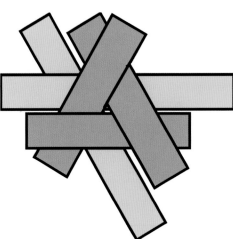

This figure is incorrect. It contains both right-pointing and left-pointing elements

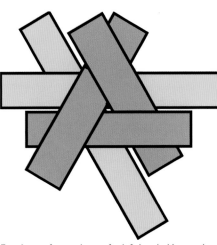

For those of you who prefer left-handed hex and mad weave constructions, here is a correct version of the left-handed triangle and the first two sets of lashers.

STEP 7

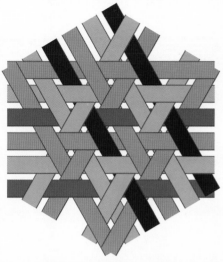

The second set of lashers completed.

STEP 8

The path of the third set of lashers.

◯ STEP 7: Complete the second set of lashers. We have only the last set of lashers to add. At this point, the partially constructed mad weave looks rather unkempt. Not to worry — you need a little wiggle room to fit in the last set of strips. You will tighten everything at the end.

◯ STEP 8: The path of the third set of strips. The pattern changes again. The right-pointing component completes the unfinished triangles, and the pattern changes to "under three strips, over three strips." This means that there is a lasher bundled with the triangle. Depending on the direction of your lashing and the handedness of your project, the directions can be either "under a lasher and a lower-level triangle, then over three strips" or "under the triangle and the first lasher thereafter, then over three strips." Whether the existing lasher is before or after the triangle can be determined by checking the handedness of each of the two alternatives.

◯ STEP 9: Finishing touches. You may wonder where the red and green triangles came from. The red ones are just along for the ride — they are made by the strips that the lasher travels over to reach the next lower-level triangle. The lashers make their own triangles as they cross over from three different directions.

STEP 9

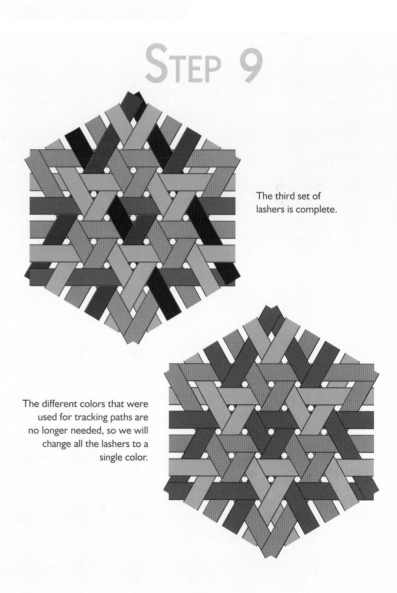

The third set of lashers is complete.

The different colors that were used for tracking paths are no longer needed, so we will change all the lashers to a single color.

Now that the weaving is done, very gently tighten the strips, working from the middle. When the strips are evenly spaced and the pertinent angles are thirty, sixty, or one-hundred-and-twenty degrees, run a thin line of glue around the circumference of the piece. Be careful not to glue the weave to the table. When the glue has dried, turn the weaving over and put a light coat of glue on the back.

You're done! Now, keep for reference!

> TIP:
>
> We have just built a hex-based mad weave. Of course, we have also created a pattern: stacked spots. Can't avoid it — any coloring that would be helpful in orienting ourselves would also create a pattern. A single-color mad weave is an advanced adventure! This nine-step process is the pattern for all hex-based mad weaves. If you are not constructing a spot form, there will be multi-colored triangles. Ignore the color. The lasher begins by either going under a lasher strip and then traveling under the triangle, or the lasher dives under the triangle and comes back after the strip on the far side of the triangle.

PATTERN FORMS

Having looked at the basic structure of mad weave, let's weave spots, stars, and tumbling blocks. The spot, tumbling block, and star, or flower, forms are the three most common forms and are relatively simple to construct. The spot form is the simplest pattern, and the stacked spots variation is the easiest to weave. You just wove one!

Small wall quilt, 7.5" x 10". *Dyeing Day at the Guild* has blue-green center spots and surrounding strips in five different colors. All of the fabric was batik, so there was a lot of color change in the individual strips. Most of the time I protected the center spots by not allowing blue or green colors to touch them.

Spots Pattern

We'll begin with the spot family of patterns. You'll see some examples of each form as well as the instructions for weaving that form.

The basic spot form is the mad weave analogy to a 2 x 2 x 2 hexagon in hex weave. There is a central hexagon in the center (the spot), surrounded by six hexagons. It is capable of great variation in colors and shading. The classic spot form is also the easiest to weave since each layer is a single color and you always know where you are.

At first, the spot pattern may seem too simplistic and lacking in energy. However, if you have a strong central spot, you can take all sorts of liberties with the surrounding colors, and the overall pattern will hold — and can become very interesting as well.

Once you allow variations in the colors of the strips surrounding the central spot, you are in an ideal environment for experimenting with color. The central spot gives stability to the composition and the surrounding colors while the variation in the other strips provides movement.

The tubes of fabric used to weave this pillow were lightly stuffed with synthetic yarn, and the three-dimensional effect is striking. Pillow approximately 14" per side.

The basic Spot Form. *Hawaiian Roses* has more than two dozen roses with lush foliage and does not require a vase. Triangular pillow approximate size, 14" per side.

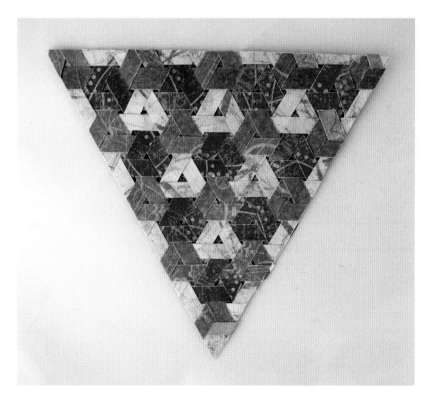

Stacked Spots

There is a special case when you use three different colors in constructing a spot-form mad weave. Instead of a single center spot, the colors alternate in being the center and the spots appear to be stacked on top of each other. This is the pattern you made when you wove your generic mad weave.

This sample uses three colors to form a stack of spots. Size: 6" on a side.

Visual Instructions for Spot Weaves

Let's begin with a spot-form mad weave. Spot form is characterized by single-color layers. The basic spot weave has only two colors. The first hex weave in this example is yellow, the second hex is red, and the lasher is also red. This will produce a mad weave with a yellow central spot, surrounded by red. The following four drawings will provide you with the information you need to construct a spot-form mad weave. For more details, please consult the directions for making a generic mad weave at the beginning of this chapter.

Hex weave for lower layer of Mad Weave, Spot Form.

Second independent hex weave for Mad Weave, Spot Form.

Layers one and two nested, Spot Form.

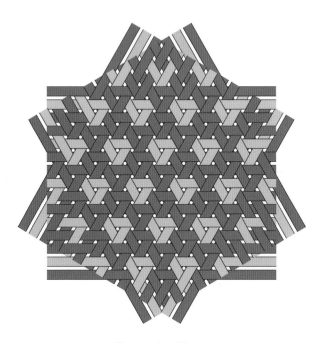

The completed figure.

The lashers are all red, so this will be a simple spot pattern. If we had made the lasher a third color, we would see stacked spots instead of isolated spots.

Tumbling Blocks Pattern

Probably the most familiar pattern is the tumbling blocks form, which looks like a series of cubes of at least three colors. As you scan across the cubes, the differences in the colors, and more importantly, the values of the colors, cause changes in which the orientation of the cube that is facing you appears to move and the blocks seem to tumble. To maximize the effect, use colors with a limited range of values, and spaced equally along the range.

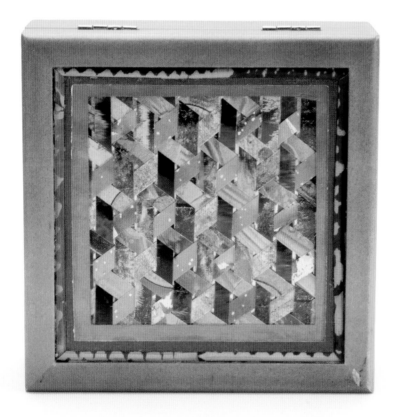

Shangri La. A small box with a more traditional tumbling-block appearance. Size: 4" square. Constructed of recycled Christmas cards. It has a lot of movement: Stare at one point for a moment and you will probably see the same point become a point on the top of another cube or a point on the side of a second cube or the bottom of a third. (If you recycle cards, make sure that there is no identifiable writing that is visible.) All three layers are identical. The horizontal, right-pointing, and left-pointing components each have a different color, but each layer has the same colors in the same places.

Close-up of a wall-hanging woven entirely of batik fabrics. You can see groups of blocks tumble together. Approximate size of sample about 6" x 4". Most people who first see this quilt-like hanging cannot believe that it is not quilted. It does look like quilting, but without the stitches. It is a very appealing pattern and you will find it in a wide variety of textile techniques.

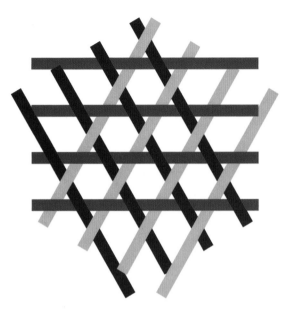

First hex weave. Mark several of the framed triangles so that you don't lose your bearing.

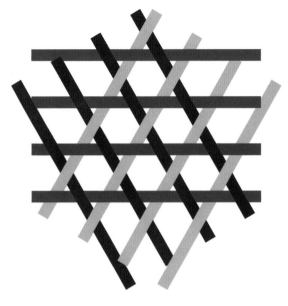

Second hex weave, same as the first.

First and second layers superimposed.

Completed figure. Use the directions for building a generic mad weave for construction details.

Star Pattern

I particularly love the star or flower form. It evokes old quilts of star-shaped flowers in a garden, with names like "Granny's Garden." Each flower has six petals and has six leaves as a border.

The Gentleman's Jewelry Box has dark stars and lighter borders. Although there is some variation in each component, it is essentially a monochromatic scheme. The image is 6" x 6".

Contrast *The Gentleman's Jewelry Box* with the dancing stars of this pillow. Although both are monochromatic, the differences in value between the strips are much greater in the black-and-white pillow. In addition, each star has a little gradient inside it that makes your eyes dance along with the stars. Approximately 17" on a side.

Sunrise was made from astronomy photographs. 6" x 6". We are not limited to two — or even seven — colors. As long as our border color is sufficiently different from the other colors that it doesn't get blended with them, you can have as many interior colors as you'd like and still have a star pattern!

Summer Dreams. Diameter approximately 11". Sometimes we want a subtler star. The clock was painted with watercolors on heavy paper, using clear hues of green, blue, and purple. Some of the strips were rinsed in water to encourage them to run and become lighter and to blend with the other colors. Other strips were repainted to become darker. Generally, the dark colors were used as borders, but the differences in hue and value were not great, and the whole piece has a nice watercolor haze. This is particularly important when we are designing clock faces. We want to have an attractive pattern, but it can't overwhelm the hands of the clock.

Constructing Stars

○ STEP 1: The first layer has two directions that are in the same color and one direction that is a second color. The second color will be the border of the flower or star.

○ STEP 2: Make a second hex weave identical to the first, and rotate it until the yellow strips are right-facing.

The second set of lashers completed.

The second set of lashers completed.

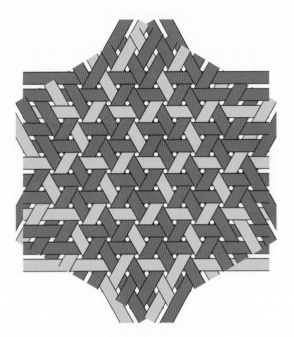

The two hex weaves are superimposed. The first layer has the border color in a left-pointing position. The second layer has the border color in the right-pointing position. The picture of the nested pair of hex weaves shows very clearly that the remaining border-color strips are to fill in the horizontal openings. It is the only direction in which the border is absent.

The completed star-form mad weave.

Stacked Stars

Stacked stars are very interesting. There are three different colored stars and three different colored borders. It is filled with movement, and the stars and blocks slip in and out of your vision. One of the many ways that you may see it is as a multiple image of three different-colored stars, each balanced by one point on its neighbor.

The secret of this pattern is that each color is repeated twice, although that is not obvious until the lashing is under way. When you rotate the second weave sixty degrees clockwise and superimpose the first one on the second, suddenly we see signs of incipient stars and clear slots denoting the places where lashers enter and leave the lower-level triangles.

There are several ways to complete the weaving. First, we know that every color is doubled in the final piece, so we can fill in the colors we know to be true. Second, we can use the instructions for the generic mad weave, which will work here as well. Third, we can work from the finished image and figure out what has to happen to get the pattern. Finally, we can work from the colors directly to get the next lasher color.

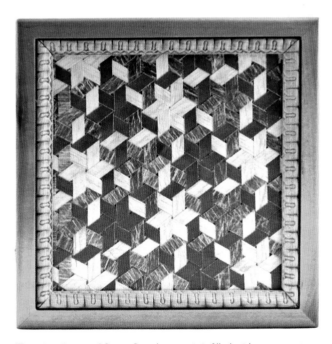

This piece is named *Dance Party* because it is filled with movement, as if we were looking down on a ballroom and watching people dancing the waltz. Size: 6" x 6". Stacked Stars are the most challenging of the simple mad weave patterns.

The lower layer of the hex weave. Note that you do not have any doubled colors.

Layer Two – still no doubled threads.

Superimposed layers.

The procedure for a situation like stacked stars, where colors keep changing layers and there is no intuitive way to check whether you are integrating the layers properly, would work better with the layered hex-weave method of constructing hex weave. Better yet, consider the alternative method of constructing mad weave presented in the next chapter. The method we are calling Diamonds are a girl's best friend is ideal for complicated patterning.

The completed stacked stars are so compelling that it is a pattern worth trying. You will encounter it again in the next chapter, using a very different mad weave procedure that is designed to simplify the weaving of complex figures.

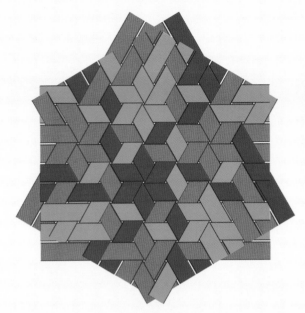

Completed stacked stars.

Note from Elizabeth Lang-Harris:

For the adventurous, the component rectangles of this mad weave are shown below. You now know enough about hex-derived mad weave to create the mad weave using the component patterns — but you don't have to. My co-author, Charlene St. John, and I have developed another way to weave mad weave. In the remainng chapters, Charlene will present Diamonds are a girl's best friend using a new method of constructing mad weave that makes it much easier to create and combine complex patterns. Have fun!

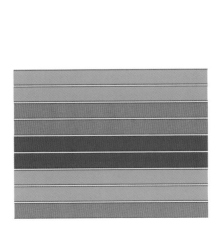

Horizontal strips. The colors are read top from bottom.

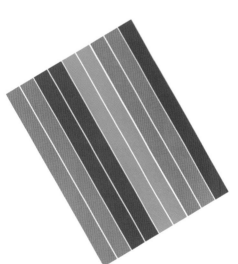

Left-pointing strips. The colors are read left from right.

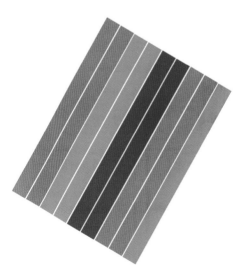

Right-pointing strips. The order of the colors here is also read from left to right.

Hex Weave and Mad-Weave Comparisons: Hearts and Triangles

All three of the hearts have the same number of strips per side, but they vary in two important respects: the width of the individual strips and the weave structure. Look at how narrow the hex strips have to be for the small hex weave to begin to approach the size of the small mad weave.

Notice the amount of information we have managed to pack into the little mad weave heart. It is pretty flexible and you can trim it easily at any point to obtain a real curve (after stabilizing it with glue or fusing it). It has two colors of strips, and was woven as a spot-form mad weave, so we have visible yellow spots.

In the triangle pattern, the holes in the hex weave are filled with strips in the mad weave. In all of the comparisons, the mad weave figure gives a lot of information about itself and is good at expressing great thoughts in small spaces. In comparison, the hex weave is a bolder pattern with the flexibility to be embellished.

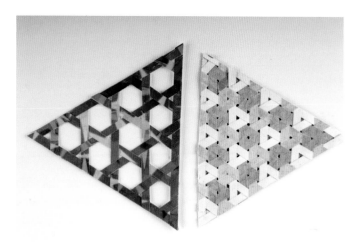

Three hearts, three different materials, two patterns. You can see pretty clearly the choices between hex weave and mad weave. Without the decorative edging, the small hex heart is approximately 3.5" x 4". The small mad weave heart is approximately 3" x 3.5". The large hex heart is about 7.25" x 8."

Triangular hex and mad weaves, both about 4" on a side.

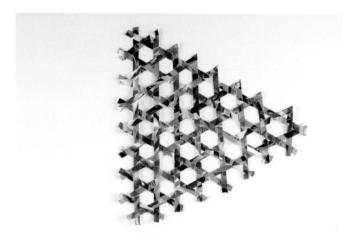

This a good-sized triangle, made from a recycled catalog cover. Approximately 9" per side.

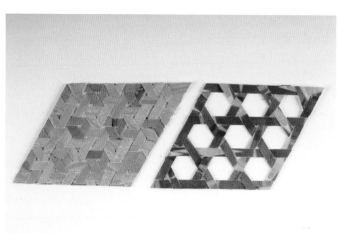

The two diamonds are the same size, both approximately 7" from point to point and 4" per side.

▒ TRIANGULAR PILLOWS

We're going to make a triangular pillow! You've seen close-ups of some of the pillows, and you'll see more patterns in the next few pages. This is the final project in the hex weave and hex-based mad weave section of this introduction to triaxial weaving, so pick a pattern and let's begin.

Almost everyone loves pillows, and a pile of beautiful pillows is enticing and comforting. Fortunately, they are quick to make and don't take a lot of material, so you can sample freely and have patterns you can really use. The center pillow has brick-red border strips and the petals are pale pink and green — or is the border made of light strips surrounding a red and green flower — or is there a green border around red and white petals? All of the above! This is a special characteristic of flower forms that have two-color petals and are properly balanced so that the colors are distributed evenly.

A snuggle of triangular pillows. The width of the strips varies from about half an inch to a full inch, but each pillow will use just one width. The length of a side varies between fourteen and seventeen inches. If a pillow looks puffy, the strips have probably been stuffed prior to weaving.

Close-up of pillow. This was actually woven as a two-color star, with the light strips as the border and the batik strips as the flower. However, there is so much movement in the batik strips that it tumbles more than it is still.

Another pillow close-up. This one has had several light strips replace dark strips. The light strips serve as boundaries and organizers.

Supplies

- ◆ Four fat quarters of fabric in two or three different patterns for the front of the pillow. Cotton fabric intended for quilting is a good place to begin, but you can use almost any fabric that doesn't fray or fall apart with handling. You can make a small triangular pillow front with 3 or 4 fat quarters.
- ◆ Material for the back of the pillow.
- ◆ Fusible interfacing, enough to cover the bottom of the completed triangle.
- ◆ Stuffing for the pillow.
- ◆ Fabric to use for holding the stuffing inside the pillow. This fabric will not be seen. If you choose to use a pre-made pillow form, wait until the pillow top is finished to make sure you have the right size.
- ◆ Stuffing for the strips. You can use scrap yarn, interfacing, un-spun pencil roving, or anything that is flexible and durable.

Instructions

○ STEP 1: Pick one of the mad weave patterns and some fabric you really love. Wash and dry the fabric. If the color runs, do not use the fabric for pillows, no matter how beautiful it is.

○ STEP 2: Put inch marks on the bars and assemble the frame to be an equilateral triangle. (You don't have to use a triangular frame, but it is so handy for making triangular shapes that I encourage you to try it.)

○ STEP 3: Cut or tear 2" strips from the fabric that is at least as long as your frame (because the fabric will be attached to the frame). The longer the better, though — you'll save time in sewing and ironing if you can get more than one strip from a tube. There's a trade-off, however, because as strips get very long, they become difficult to turn right side out.

○ STEP 4: Fold a strip in half, right sides together, and sew a 1/4" seam. You now have an inside-out tube (like spaghetti-straps).

○ STEP 5: Turn the strip right-side out and press it. Stuff the strip if you want a puffy pillow.

For *Granny's Garden*, after I had turned the strips right-side out, I pressed them flat and then ran two extra seams, one down each side of the strip. The whole effect is more tailored and the little valleys provide some extra texture.

We will first create two separate hex weaves and then lash them together.

○ STEP 6: Separate the strips for each layer.

○ STEP 7: Cut a strip that is about 4" longer than one side of your frame.

○ STEP 8: Attach the ends of the strip to the frame under a little tension using clamps, brads, or staples. Whatever works!

Before you fasten down the next strip, think about where you will put it. We know that there will have to be two more strips added between adjacent hex strips, so you will leave a space between the strips that is equal to twice the width of the strip.

○ STEP 9: Repeat for each strip. Since this is a triangle, each strip is shorter than the strip before, and you will probably end up pairing two or three short strips with one of the longer strips in a single tube. You might want to keep a record of the fabric, so you have good data about the amount of fabric needed for different projects.

Once you have completed the first layer of the first hex weave, put the second layer on top of the frame. Remember that the first and second layers never interact with each other, but depend on the lashers to connect them. If you are having difficulty holding your angles, try one of the alignment tools listed in the Appendix.

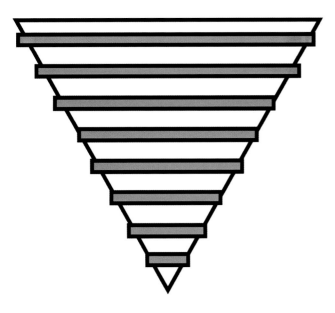

Your frame should look something like this after the first layer has been finished.

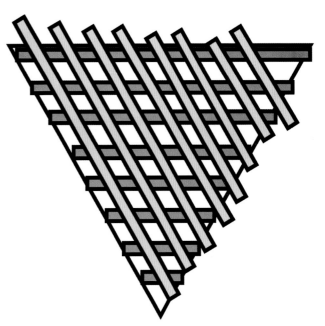

After adding the second layer, your frame should look something like this. The frame so far has horizontal and left-pointing elements, and needs the right-pointing elements to complete.

You can start weaving in the third layer almost anywhere, but the middle is probably easiest. The lashers all weave over the gold strips and under the strips of purple. If you remember that the bottom strips are pulled up and the upper strips are being pushed down and that you are using a right-handed lasher, you should have very little difficulty with this step. The plain weave rule applies here since we are at this point weaving a hex, so, if you start in the middle of the hex fabric, begin by weaving under a purple strip, over a gold, under a purple, over a gold, and so on. Attach strips to the frame as is helpful.

Making Two Hex Weaves

If you have two sets of stretcher frames, and one is sufficiently small enough to fit inside the other, you can make the two hex weaves, leave them on their frames, and weave them together without dislodging anything. If you have a single set, take the first one off the frame very carefully and leave the second one on the frame. Lash the two hexes together, following the instructions for the hex-based mad weave and paying attention to the color sequences of the pattern you have chosen.

Finishing

Once the weaving is complete, you will want to stabilize it — or your strips will start falling out, especially the short pieces. Pin all the strips on the periphery to more stable strips, as they tend to fall out if not constrained.

If your frame is wood and can handle the heat of the iron, fuse the back of the weave to one-sided fusible interfacing or, using two-sided interfacing, fuse the back of the weave to a piece of cloth. The backing cloth will not be seen. Remove the new mad weave carefully from the frame — some of the edge pieces will likely not be as well-fused as the center, so re-fuse as necessary.

If your frame is not wood, don't touch the iron to it unless you are sure there will be no damage to the frame or your iron. Instead, pin the end strips securely to the others, carefully release the weaving from the frame, and fuse it to a protective backing as soon as possible.

You now have a pillow top. You will need to add a back of the same size, fiberfill for stuffing the pillow (make a slightly smaller interior pillow to hold the stuffing), an optional zipper, and decorative cording, if desired, but congratulations...you have come a long way since that first star.

Now that you have a little experience with hex-based mad weave, let's compare the hex weave and mad weave

() MAD WEAVE is considerably denser than hex weave, about three times as dense. This makes sense since mad weave can be made from three hex weaves. (There are some technical aspects that together might argue that mad weave would be a little more than three times as dense, but for our purposes, we will use three.) This difference in density has implications.

() HEX WEAVE drapes better than mad weave.

() MAD WEAVE can hold more information than hex weave. Remember how big some of the figures were when we made them in hex weave? We can greatly condense the size of our figure by using mad weave.

() MAD WEAVE uses three times as much material as hex weave, so if you are working with something precious, you might want to make a hex weave and attach it to a backing fabric.

() It's easier to hide replacement or embellishment strips in the center of the fabric in MAD WEAVE.

() It's more fun to embellish HEX WEAVE. The tempting open spaces of hex weave are filled in with the additional strips used in mad weave.

Bending the Rules

Compared to hex weave, mad weave is quite dense, which means that you can take liberties with the construction that you can't with hex weave. One of my favorite ways of bending the rules is to build a mad weave and remove strips to expose part of the lower layer.

Rush Hour was woven with hand-dyed strips of heavy watercolor paper. 6" square. This piece is filled with happy movement and is reminiscent of people dashing around to prepare for a celebration. Removing some of the strips can create long floats, but it also introduces added texture.

A lot of artists felt that they needed to create memorials marking the day that the Twin Towers were attacked. Incomplete patterns can be very powerful. In *Nine-Eleven*, I tried to capture the chaos as the world as we knew it fell apart. This piece was constructed using commercial paper and backed with fire-colored foil. 6" square.

Mixing strips of different widths gives you even more opportunities to play with color and movement. A thinner strip can show the color of the strip beneath it, giving you the chance to blend more colors. As you scan across the fabric, the occasional thin strip breaks the pattern, like a little syncopated note.

Changing the Pattern

Changing the patterning of the strip itself can make unusual variations. Both January Morning and Harvest Festival were woven with doubled strips.

In January Morning, I paired each red strip with a lighter, more heavily patterned strip and taped the two together lengthwise. (You can purchase ribbon already configured this way.) It was woven with the light strips on the outside, so that each red pinwheel is surrounded by a swirl of snow.

Harvest Festival was woven in exactly the same way, except that the darker side of the double ribbon became the outside. The overall patterns look like they are related, but they also look very different. The red pinwheels of January Morning look like they are separate from the snow and are floating a little above it, whereas in Harvest Festival the pinwheel and its brown border appear more attached.

January Morning was woven from paper designed on the computer and printed directly onto heavy watercolor paper. 6" square.

Harvest Festival was woven from paper designed on the computer, and then printed and hand-painted. 6" square.

Embellishment

Mad weave does not lend itself to embellishment as easily as hex weave, but, for diehard embellishers, there are ways!

The simplest way is to leave a little extra space between strips so that the backing paper can be glimpsed. If you use a backing with some kind of glitter, a little glitz can add a big sparkle to your work.

If you weave a little loosely, you can add extra strips by sliding the new strip into the path of an existing strip. With one end of the new strip anchored, you can do anything you want with the other. Make basketry curls, silk ribbon embroidery, or duplicate stitch.

Don't forget the beads! You can run your wire or thread under the strips and it won't be seen.

Revisiting Hex Topics

Let's take a moment to review some of the topics covered in the last seven chapters. Generally, the conclusions made for hex weave hold for hex-based mad weave as well, though there are a few additions to make.

◇ COLOR: Generally, color will take precedence over structure and texture, even though texture usually will dominate structure. This is what enables triaxial weaves to look so different despite the fact they are structurally the same. It also means that if you want to emphasize patterns in your work, keep to solid colors with very little texture. Ribbons are ideal for pattern work, and you will see many beautiful examples in the next chapter.

Spots form mad weave using hand-painted paper and heavily embellished with beads. Size: 6" square.

◇ GRADIENTS: Gradients and the interaction among components can be much more effective in mad weave than in hex weave. The very density of mad weave encourages color blending.

◇ BULL'S EYES (see images next page): The paper set-up looked like the paper in the second example of hex-weave bull's eye (page 35). The paper had blues and teals on either side of a broad pink stripe. We had concluded that this paper arrangement would work for a single bull's eye, and this is what happens here. It looks more complete than the hex version because the fabric is denser.

The hexagon on the next page is another mad weave using paper painted with a center stripe; in this case, the stripe is white and the legs are blue. Once a round showed more blue than white, I finished it off and then glued it over a hex weave bull's eye. It's quite effective.

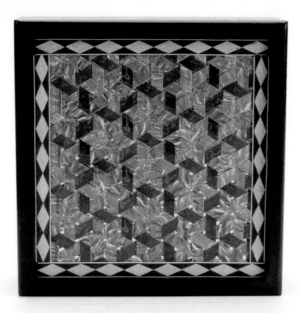

Poinsettia is a treasure box with a strong red-to-green gradient and a marquetry border. Size: 6" square.

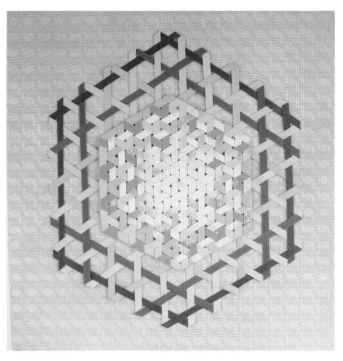

The pink-centered clock was made from hand-painted, hand-cut, heavy watercolor paper. Approximately 10" in diameter.

Another faux bull's eye variation, measuring 12" square.

Aunt Sukey's Garden
This project demonstrates much of what we've done so far.

Imagine a garden with the flowers growing along the fence. You can look through the fence and see a soft blue and pink spring sunset. This picture, **Aunt Sukey's Garden**, illustrates many of the ideas that have been presented so far.

There are three different widths of strips: 1/2", 3/8", and 1/4". The sky is the largest, the fence is second, and the flowers have the narrowest strips. Combining strips of different sizes adds texture and depth. The gate was a large hex weave, about 12" x 18", and was the base weave. It framed the sky and, in turn, was framed by the flowers.

Most of the flowers are glued on, but some have lower legs inserted into the paths of the fence strips to anchor them. More interesting is the section where the mad weave was woven directly on the gate. The gate served as the lower layer, a second hex weave was positioned on top of the gate, and a third set of strips did the lashing.

Aunt Sukey's Garden. Hand-painted, hand-cut, heavy watercolor paper, marquetry frame. Approximate size, 13" x 19".

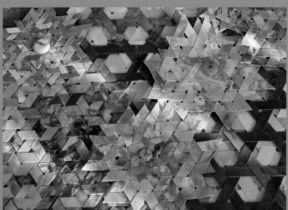

This close-up gives a better view of individual strips and shows the embellishments more clearly. The purple plant nestled in the crook of the brighter plants was one of the sections that were woven directly onto the gate. Only the centers of the flowers were glued down, so that the petals could open and spread a little, again giving it greater texture and dimensionality. There are bead centers to the flowers, and the beads sit on individual hex units.

TWILL-BASED MAD WEAVE

Mad weave is maddening, fascinating, structured, and yet allows endless creativity. If you worked your way through the hex weave portion of this book, you learned that you could create some amazing layered hex-based mad weaves. However, for more complex color mad weave patterns and tapestries, a twill weave method that easily allows creation of the mad weave fabric without building in layers is more advantageous. Luckily, with "Diamonds are a girls best friend," we have just such a method. We will cover it in detail when we work through the first pattern.

Color is used to generate a staggering number of patterns and designs. Basic structure, along with the "Diamonds are a girl's best friend" method, is covered in the Tumbling Blocks pattern. We will move on to other patterns from there.

◤ MATERIALS AND WORK SURFACES

Supplies

Most of the following basic supplies are easily available with little or no expenditure of cash: Pins, a needle with a big eye, shears, index card with the end cut at a 30° angle, piece of cork board or sheet foam to use as a work surface, and strips of fabric of equal width to weave with.

However, as you get more involved in making mad weave projects, consider acquiring some of these materials.

◊ CURLING RIBBON: This is a great choice for samples, cards, and experimenting. It is flexible, inexpensive, and comes in a wide variety of colors, textures, and finishes. I did a series of double-sided window-hangings out of acetate/metallic Christmas ribbons, so don't limit yourself!

- **Satin ribbon**, both single- and double-sided and in any width. Double-sided is a little easier to work with simply because you don't have to worry which side ends up. There are some really great printed single-side satin ribbon that is well worth taking the time to work with. Don't forget picot edged.

- **Grosgrain ribbon** is marvelous. Plain, striped, printed — it adds great texture to your creation.
- **Silk ribbon** is the ribbon of choice if you like to dye your own ribbon. Think color gradations.

◊ PAPER: It can be thin, thick, solid-colored, printed, double-sided, or custom-painted. It just can't be too fragile or it will tear and crinkle as you try to weave with it.

◊ FABRIC: Be creative. I used good quality quilting cotton folded and/or sewn into tubes for the quilted project pieces.

Tools of the Trade

○ GOOD, LONG STRAIGHT PINS. These are used to secure the ribbons to the work surface. Pick the kind that is easiest for you to handle. If you plan on working with satin ribbon, you will be securing your finished creation to fusible interfacing with an iron. Make sure your pins either are all metal or have glass heads. (Plastic heads can melt onto the iron.) I advise against T-headed pins — they just seem to get in the way and tangle with each other.

○ A COUPLE PAIR OF SHARP SCISSORS. You should have one for cloth and one for paper. Good thread scissors work very well on ribbons.

○ YARN NEEDLES and/or 5" WEAVING NEEDLES. Important: Both styles have dull points.

○ FUSIBLE INTERFACING. For securing fabric and non-paper ribbons. HTC-Retail fusi-knit® is my recommended brand as it is one of the few fusible interfacing fabrics that bonds well to satin ribbon.

○ A 30°/60° TRIANGLE (mine is plastic). These are available at most quilting and craft stores.

Work surface.

Work Surface

The work surface is an important consideration and you will probably need to make it yourself. Each strip in every layer of mad weave has to be securely pinned down. I have used a child's small-framed chalk-board and/or grease-board, which I glued thin sheet foam to, for making photo-size pieces. For larger pieces, 1/2" polystyrene insulation sheets (available at home improvement centers) and foam core (available at arts and crafts stores) each work well as a work surface.

A sheet of muslin that is cut 4" bigger than the board provides an excellent cover for either. Wrap the muslin tightly over the front surface of the board and secure it on the back with staples and/or clear packing tape. A 12" x 18" board is a handy working size. Use a straight edge and pencil to mark a single line down the long center of the board. Using your 30° angle, mark two crosses that run across the full width of the board.

TWILL-BASED MAD WEAVE
9:BASIC PATTERNS

In this chapter, we will work through some of the basic patterns with plenty of tips on construction. As you become more familiar with mad weave, you might find the pattern listing in the appendix gives you all the information you need to produce a given pattern.

The details of using the Diamonds are a girl's best friend method are included in the first pattern, "Tumbling Blocks." This system is an absolute gem when you require more control over color placement of each weaver than you can get from the interlocking hex weave system developed by co-author Elizabeth Lang-Harris and her husband Richard Harris. Elizabeth and I developed Diamonds are a girl's best friend as we dove deeper and deeper into mad weave madness.

I encourage you to make — and save — lots of samples. Yes, right away! Each color combination offers something new. Make samples of basic patterns and purposely misplace colors within a pattern, add new colors as you subtract others, or combine two patterns in the same piece. Use different tones of the same color and then do the same pattern with complementary colors. Let yourself play and explore. Saving these samples is how your personal reference library will be built. A loose-leaf binder with plastic sleeves works very well.

Some notes on structure for weavers. For left-handed mad weave, the structure is essentially an over 1, under 2 twill weave from the right and an over 2, under 1 twill structure from the left. It's just the opposite for right-hand mad weave. Unlike hex-based mad weave, you don't need to get too caught up in the technicalities at this point. Unless you plan to make two images that mirror each other, for most mad weavers, it is simply a point of interest.

In twill-based mad weave, the terminology will change from the terminology used in layered hex mad weave, mostly in regards to the definition of a layer. In twill-based mad weave, a layer constitutes all weavers going in a particular direction, be it vertical, lower right to upper left, or lower left to upper right. In weaving, this would be similar to the warp, the weft, and a supplemental weft.

TUMBLING BLOCKS PATTERN

We will set up the work surface for a 4" x 6" sample card. Pin a 4"x 6" index card to the center of the work surface before you begin weaving. Since the center of the reference lines on the work surface have now been covered up, use a pencil and a straight edge to transfer the base line and 30° lines onto the card. I am going to assume that paper or paper ribbon is the weaving material. It is often easier to use a narrow strip of double-sided tape at each end of the sample card, to which the first layer of strips can be stuck, rather than using pins. For layers two and three, the ends of the weavers will be pinned at the edge of the card. When the weaving is completed, and the pins are removed, the edges are secured by taping them to the card.

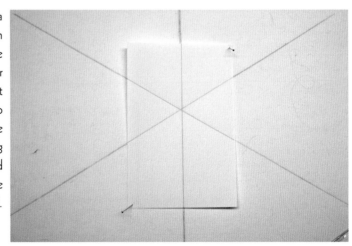

Fix card to surface.

STEP 1: Cut weavers of one color and secure them to the board, side by side, aligned with the line you drew down the center of your work surface. Leave a tiny amount of space between your weavers so that you have room to weave in the other two layers.

STEP 2: Cut the second layer of weavers in a different color. We will start making use of the diamonds on this layer. Weave in the first strip making sure that it travels over one strip and then under two strips of the first layer. Align it with one of the 30° lines that you drew on your work surface and pin it down. Look at the accompanying diagram and then weave in the second strip. It will also travel over one strip of the first layer and then under two strips. This is a 1 / 2 twill weave pattern.

ACCURACY CHECK:

This is the first place where the diamonds are your best friends. Make sure the individual diamonds are touching by the points of their long axes. (Think of it as the first diamond pointing to where the next diamond goes.) If the diamonds are not lined up properly — the fat sides of the diamonds are touching — you only need to remove and re-weave the second strip.

STEP 3: Weave in the rest of the strips of this layer, constantly referring to the diamonds for correct placement. Stick with the over one, under two twill weaving pattern. Keep the weavers laying parallel to the reference lines. You'll see why this is so important when you start the third layer.

ACCURACY CHECK:

Rotate the piece until you see the diamonds you just created are lined up vertically. If it looks a little skewed, you didn't lay the second layer in at a 30° angle to the strips in the first layer. Take the time to get all the strips lined up with the reference lines now. Don't be surprised if just two angled reference lines are not enough. You may find that you often need multiple reference lines.

STEP 4: Cut the final weavers in a third color. A yarn needle will make weaving ribbons easier. Look for a long diamond with a small diamond on each side of it. See the diagram. Insert your weaver (see highlighted strip) behind the lower right edge of the diamond of your choice. It will travel under three strips, pop back up to the surface, travel over three strips and dive back down. Continue

(Step 4 is pictured on following page)

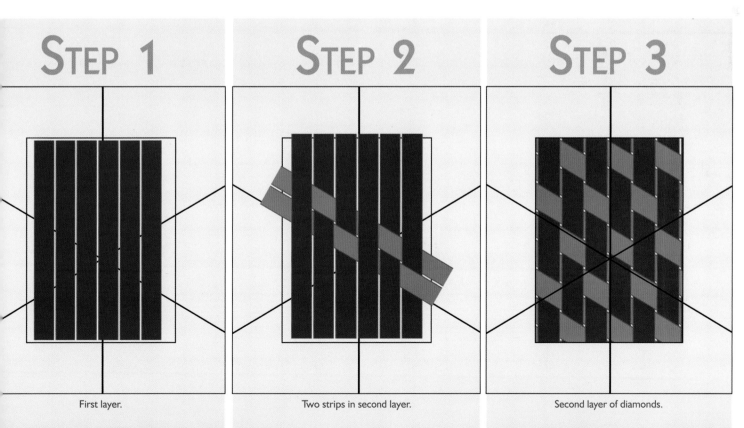

STEP 1	STEP 2	STEP 3
First layer.	Two strips in second layer.	Second layer of diamonds.

TECHNICAL NOTE:

Getting to know your weave structure is how you will be able to branch out and be creative. It will also make finding and correcting those pesky mistakes a lot easier. Look at the strips you have just woven together. As a weaver goes under three strips, it is actually going under one strip of the first layer and two strips of the second layer. When it comes back to the surface, it will go over two strips of the first layer and one strip of the second layer. When you focus on just the interaction of the third layer with the first layer you can see an over 2, under 1 twill pattern. When you focus on just the third layer strip weaving through the second layer, you can see the familiar over 1, under 2 twill.

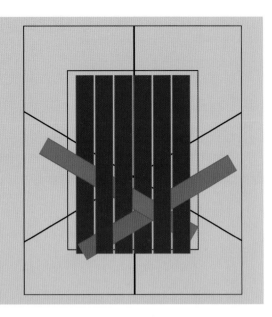

across the row. If you started with a diamond in the middle, go back and weave in the tail of your strip in the other direction. You will notice that often there are incomplete patterns along the edges of your work — that is absolutely okay.

◊ STEP 5: Continue weaving in the strips of the final layer until finished. Compare to the drawing. If your sample looks incomplete, look to see if you have missed a row. Still not quite right? You already checked layers one and two as you finished them. Now you just need to review layer three, strip by strip. All okay now? Good. Let's get this finished into a usable sampler or, better yet, since 4" x 6" is a common size, use it as an insert in a photo-display greeting card.

◊ STEP 6: Carefully remove the pins from one side of the index card. Use a long strip of cellophane tape to secure the ends of the strips that were just freed. Be sure to overlap the edge of the card stock. Do each of the remaining sides the same way. Neatly trim the sides to the edge of the card stock. If you used double-sided tape to hold down the first layer of weavers, your sample will still be attached to the card stock, which is great.

STEP 4

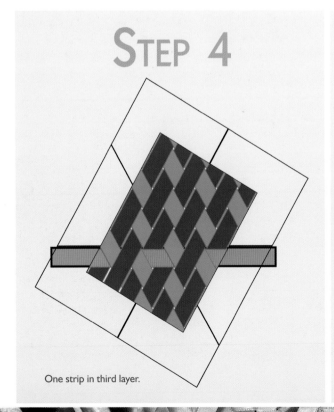

One strip in third layer.

STEPS 5-6

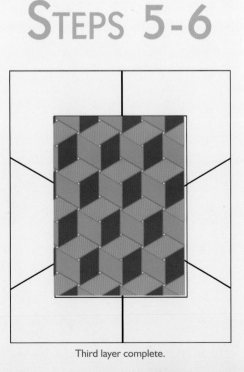

Third layer complete.

I often will go back, at this point, and run a strip of cellophane along the edge of a sample so that half the width of it is hanging off the edge. This way I can fold it around to the back of the card stock for greater security.

Congratulations! You now have a tumbling block mad weave sampler using the Diamonds are a girl's best friend method!

Tumbling blocks collage.

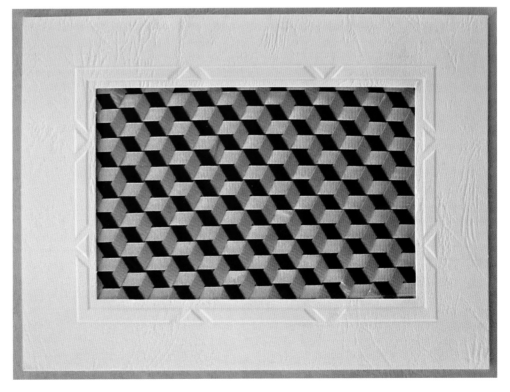

Tumbling blocks card.

STACKED SPOTS PATTERN

Like many mad weave patterns, stacked spots are a three-weaver pattern repeat. The pattern is the same for all three layers: one dark-colored, one medium-colored, one light-colored strip.

○ STEP 1: Secure the first layer to the work surface with the strips parallel to the (base) line you drew down the center of your work surface.

○ STEP 2: Start the second layer with the dark-colored weaver since it is easiest to see. Weave the 1/2 twill pattern with this strip going over the strip to the left of a dark-color weaver in the first layer and then under the next two strips. Where the dark-colored weavers from each of the two layers meet should look like an arrowhead.

○ STEP 3: Now weave in a medium-colored strip. Using the 1/2 twill pattern — weaving over one and under two — this time the "over one" will go over the strip to the left of the medium-colored strip in the first layer.

○ STEP 4: Weave in all of the strips for the second layer following the one dark-colored, one medium-colored, one light-colored pattern. Recall that this is a three-ribbon pattern repeat. You can refer back to the first strip to see how the fourth weaver goes.

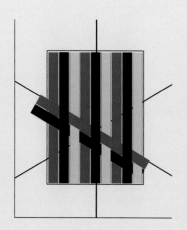

Two strips of second layer.

STEPS 1-3

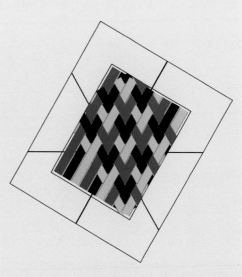

Second layer.

STEP 4

Weaving in the third layer will make the spots appear, but only if the color strips are placed properly. Turn your work surface so that the diamonds are stacked. The third layer will weave in horizontally. We will start weaving with a dark-colored strip again.

○ STEP 5: Look for a long light diamond that is flanked by small dark- and light-colored diamonds. These are the three target strips that you will weave under; then up and over the next three strips. You probably will start in the middle, so go back and weave in the tail of your dark-colored weaver.

STEP 5

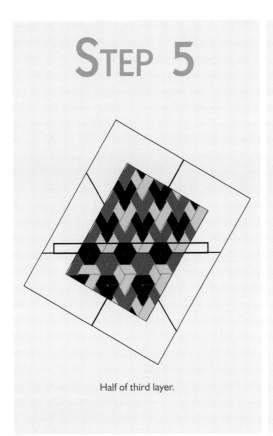

Half of third layer.

STEP 6

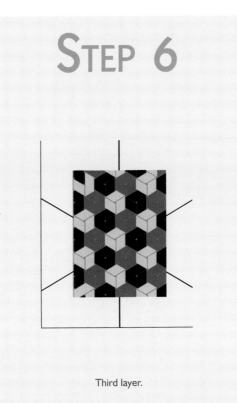

Third layer.

If you look carefully, you can see that the dark-colored weaver shows on the surface in the middle of the dark V. For a medium-colored weaver, look for a long dark-colored diamond flanked by dark- and medium-colored small diamonds to get started. For the light-colored weaver, look for a long medium-colored diamond flanked by medium- and light-colored diamonds.

The fourth ribbon goes in just like the first ribbon. (Remember, this is a three-ribbon pattern repeat.)

◇ STEP 6: Continue in this manner for the whole third layer, completing the Stacked Spots sampler.

Stacked spots collage. The pink and purple card is called the tiara pattern. It has the same three-color repeat except that the third layer was inserted off by one place. It was a happy "mistake"!

Like many mad weave patterns, Spots is another three-weaver pattern repeat. The pattern to make floating dark spots is the same for all three layers: one dark-colored and two light-colored strips.

○ STEP 1: Secure the first layer to the work surface with the strips parallel to the line you drew down the center of your work surface.

○ STEP 2: This pattern starts like stacked spots. Weave the 1/2 twill pattern with a dark-colored weaver going over the strip to the left of a dark-colored strip in the first layer, then under the next two. A dark-colored V will form where the dark-colored weaver goes under the dark-colored strip in the first layer. Now, weave in the two light-colored strips. Use the 1/2 twill pattern and align your diamonds.

○ STEP 3: Weave in all of the strips for the second layer following the one dark-colored, two light-colored pattern. Recall that this is a three-ribbon pattern repeat. You can refer back to the first strip to see where the fourth weaver goes.

○ STEP 4: Our aim in the third layer is to complete the three-sided dark spot. Each "V" is the first two sides of a spot. Pick one V to focus on. It is made of one long diamond and one smaller diamond. The dark-colored weaver that will complete the spot will go over the long dark-colored diamond and under the small diamond. Remember that on the third layer you will be weaving under three and then over three strips — so if you know the first strip to weave under is the small dark-colored diamond, then you know to also go under the next two strips. See the diagram.

(Step 4 is pictured on following page)

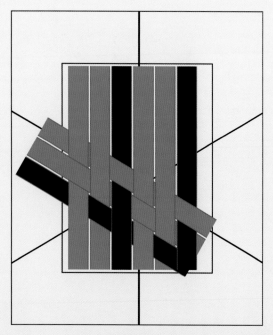

STEPS 1-2

Spots, partial second layer.

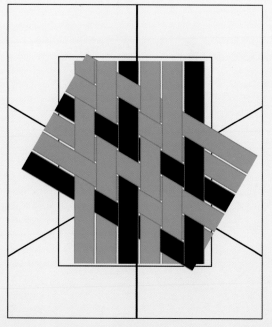

STEP 3

Spots, second layer.

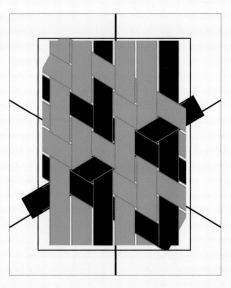

Spots, partial third layer.

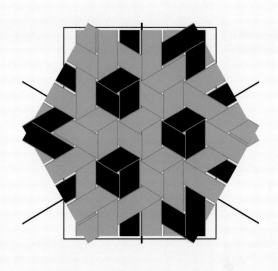

Spots, third layer.

○ STEP 5: Once you have that first strip in place, follow the diamonds and go on to weave in the two light-colored strips.

○ STEP 6: The fourth ribbon, which is dark, follows the same path as the first ribbon. (Remember, this is a three-ribbon pattern repeat.)

ACCURACY CHECK:

The first and fourth strips should have created the solid colored spots. If not, without removing any strips, look for a V that you created when you wove in the second layer. Put your finger on the third layer, light-colored strip that accidentally went into the place the dark-colored weaver belongs. Feed a dark-colored strip in, right on top of the light-colored strip. Carefully remove the light-colored strip from underneath. Make any corrections to the other three strips the same way.

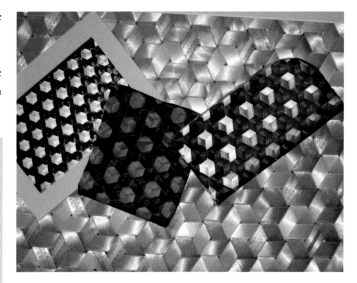

Spots collage.

○ STEP 7: Now, finish up the sampler with the same one dark, two light pattern to create the dark spots.

PINWHEEL PATTERN

This is an interesting pattern with lots of movement. It has a spot as the center of each pinwheel, but the method used to build the pinwheel is different from the one we used for spots. The color repeat for pinwheels is the same for all three layers: one dark-colored, one light-colored strip.

○ STEP 1: Secure the first layer to the work surface with the strips parallel to the (base)line you drew down the center of your work surface.

○ STEP 2: Weaving in the 1/2 twill pattern, start anywhere with either color. (Really!) Use the 1/2 twill pattern and align your diamonds. Continue for another three or four strips, alternating between light and dark. No real pattern is visible until you have four or five strips woven in.

ACCURACY CHECK:

Stop here to make sure the individual diamonds are touching by their long axis (pointing to each other). You should see the start of big zigzag stripes.

○ STEP 3: Weave in all of the strips for the second layer following the one dark-colored, one light-colored weaver pattern. Big, continuous, zigzag stripes will be visible.

○ STEP 4: For the third layer, we just have to remember that diamonds are a girls best friend. Look for any long diamond that has a small diamond on each side. These are the three strips to weave under, then over three, etc. It doesn't matter which color you weave with or where you start! As long as you weave alternating dark and light-colored strips, the pattern will develop accurately.

Pinwheels collage.

STEPS 1-3

Second layer.

STEP 4

Third layer.

Stars are a three-weaver pattern repeat. The color repeat is the same for all three layers: one dark-colored strip and then two light-colored strips.

- ◇ STEP 1: Secure the first layer to the work surface with the strips parallel to the (base)line you drew down the center of your work surface. The sample shows the strips properly laid out with an extra dark-colored ribbon at the end to frame what will become light-colored stars.

- ◇ STEP 2: It is easiest to start the second layer with a dark-colored strip. The dark-colored strip always goes over the dark-colored strip of the first layer and under the two light-colored strips. Weave in the second strip, which will be light-colored.

> **ACCURACY CHECK:**
>
> Make sure the second layer strips are aligned with one of the 30° lines that you have drawn on the work surface and the individual diamonds are touching by their long axis. If the diamonds are not aligned properly, remove the light-colored weaver and try again.

- ◇ STEP 3: Weave in all of the strips for the second layer following the one dark, two light pattern. Remember, this is a three-ribbon pattern repeat. If need be, refer to the first strip to see where the fourth weaver goes.

> **ACCURACY CHECK:**
>
> Do you have vertical stripes, as shown in the diagram?

- ◇ STEP 4 (see diagram next page): Weaving in the third layer will make the stars appear, but only if the color strips are placed properly. We will start with a dark-colored strip again. Look for a long dark-colored diamond (made from a first layer strip). It will be flanked by two smaller light-colored diamonds. Weave in the dark-colored strip. See how the dark-colored strip of the third layer went under the dark-colored strip of the first layer? The second weaver, a light-colored one, will go right next to the dark-colored strip. Look for a long light-colored diamond flanked by a regular-sized dark-colored diamond and a light-colored diamond. These are the three strips to weave under. The third weaver is also light-colored. Again look for a large

(Step 4 is pictured on following page)

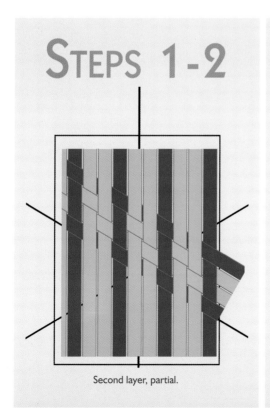

Second layer, partial.

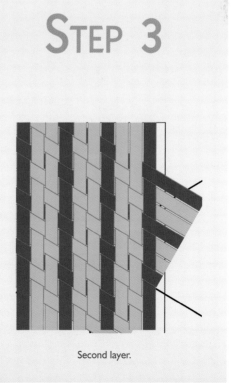

Second layer.

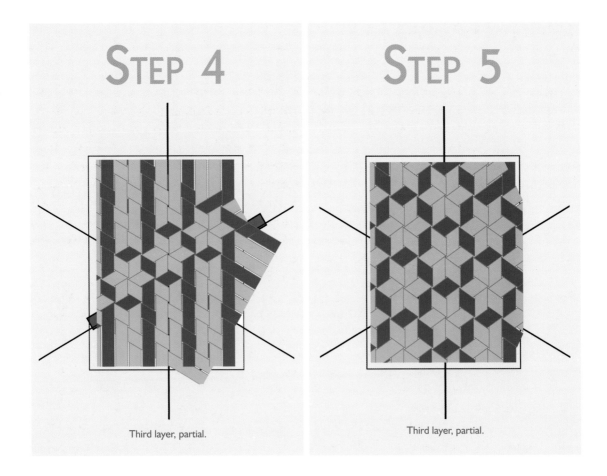

STEP 4

STEP 5

Third layer, partial.

Third layer, partial.

light-colored diamond flanked by a regular-sized light-colored diamond and a dark-colored diamond. (Just opposite of the last row.) These are the three strips to weave under. The fourth ribbon goes in just like the first ribbon. (Remember, this is a three-ribbon pattern repeat.) You can refer back three ribbons to see where to put this strip.

ACCURACY CHECK:

With these four strips on the final layer in place, a row of stars will be visible. If not, look to see if you missed a row. Fill it in with the proper color strip and make any necessary adjustments to the other ribbons. If all the strips are in place and you still cannot see the stars, look to see if your initial dark-colored strip is in the correct position. See diagram.

◇ STEP 5: Weave in the rest of the layer to complete the stars sampler.

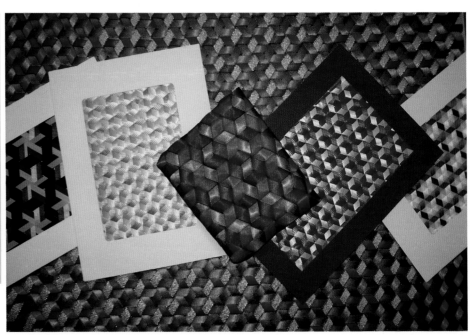

Stars montage.

Dancing stars is also a three-weaver pattern repeat. The pattern is the same for all three layers: two dark-colored, two medium-colored, two light-colored strip.

○ STEP 1: Secure the first layer to the work surface with the strips parallel to the (base)line you drew down the center of your work surface.

Focus on one pair of dark-colored weavers in the first layer. Start weaving the second layer with a dark-colored weaver. When woven in, it will always go over the right-hand dark-colored weaver in the first layer and then under the next two weavers. Pin it down aligned with one of the 30° lines you have marked on your work surface.

○ Step 2: Now, the second dark-colored weaver. Remember, the existing diamonds will point to where the diamonds of the next strip will be located. The tip for stars is that the two same-colored strips in the second layer will each go over similar colored strips from the first layer forming the beginning of the stars. See the diagram. Although it seems there is no pattern where dark goes over medium or light colors strips, the four dark-colored weavers will always form a parallelogram and the center of the dark-colored stars can be seen.

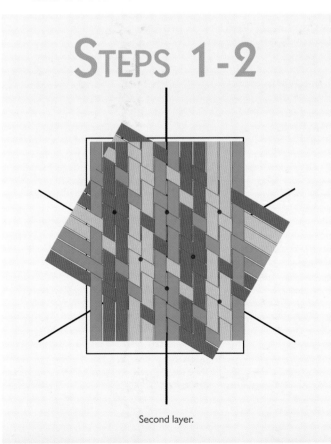

STEPS 1-2

Second layer.

To choose the next weaver color, look to see where the diamonds are pointing. In the sample here, the next pair of weavers are medium-colored. As the first dark-colored weaver always went over the right-hand dark-colored weaver in the first layer, the first medium-colored weaver always goes over the right-hand medium-colored strip in the bottom layer and the second medium-colored weaver goes over the other medium-colored strip of the bottom layer. Weave them in and do an accuracy check. The four medium-colored weavers form parallelograms and the center of the medium-colored stars can be seen.

○ STEP 3: Time to put in the third pair of weavers. In the sample, they are light-colored. The four light-colored weavers form parallelograms and the center of the light-colored stars can be seen.

○ STEP 4: Continue the 2, 2, 2 pattern until the second layer is complete.

ACCURACY CHECK:

Is the weaving scattered with dark-, medium-, and light-colored parallelograms? Have you figured out yet that if the second layer isn't lined up properly, it's really hard to weave in the third layer?

As with the previous pattern, weaving in the third layer will make the stars appear, but only if the color strips are placed properly. We will start with completing a dark-colored star. To help you focus on one dark-colored parallelogram, stick a straight pin right in the middle where the four ribbons meet. This is where the first star will form. Now, diamonds will still work for you, so rotate your work so that the final weavers will go in horizontally and the diamonds appear to be stacked in columns. Look for a long dark-colored diamond that is right next to the pin you stuck in the middle of the dark-colored parallelogram. It will be flanked by two smaller light-colored diamonds. This is your starting point.

The second dark-colored strip will go right next to the first and it will also go under a long dark-colored diamond. The third and fourth strips are medium-colored and will go right next to a medium-colored strip. The two light-colored strips are next.

○ STEP 5: Finish weaving the third layer. Technically, there will be a row of dark-colored stars alternating with multicolored stars, a row of light-colored stars alternating with multicolored stars, and, finally, a row of alternating medium and multicolored stars.

Visually, you may just see a blend of colors at first. If you used a dark color that is much darker than the other colors, those dark-colored stars will be very apparent or you will see triangles or, perhaps, both. From a distance, this pattern often resembles a quilting pattern.

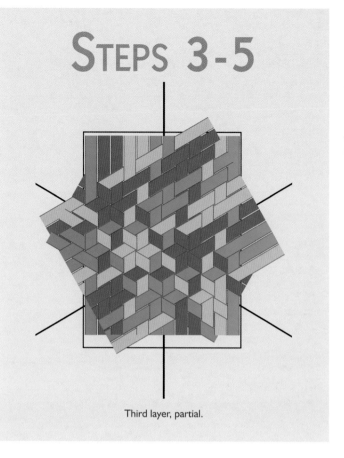

STEPS 3-5

Third layer, partial.

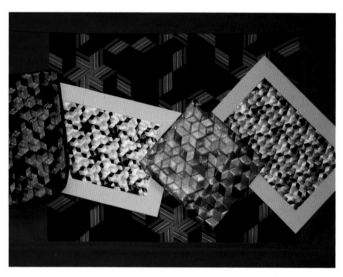

Dancing Stars montage.

Two-tone ribbons.

TWILL-BASED MAD WEAVE
10: MANDALAS

A mandala is chiefly a concentric configuration of geometric shapes. In other words, it has a central focal point and the design flows out from there in a radial fashion. The layout can be symmetrical or not. The colors can be symmetrical or not. It is entirely possible to have multiple mandalas within one work. If you want the "rays" of one mandala to intersect with the center of another mandala, use two strips in each direction to create the center of the first mandala. Move it around on your work surface until you find the point where the rays are pointing to where the next mandalas should go.

If you want multiple mandalas with different colored centers, make the centers for each mandala. Move them around on your work surface until the "rays" do not intersect the centers of the other mandalas inappropriately. (You will have to decide what is appropriate or not.) It is a little harder to do than you might first think, but the results can be spectacular.

When I first started triaxial weaving, I did lots and lots of samples. I wasn't interested in making only perfect samples either. I purposely misplaced colors so I could see what the results would be, and when I started making more major works, they were mandalas. Possibly that is why I learned the structure of mad weave so well and so early — I was weaving in new strips from all three directions as I created instead of a layer at a time. Mandalas are wonderful opportunities to be spontaneously creative, and having the skill set to make them is essential — and empowering. Feel your way by making some small samples. Let flowers, sun bursts, rainbows, quilts, and tile patterns inspire you. Find patterns developing under your fingers as you weave and follow them where they lead. Pay attention to the twill weaves and follow the diamonds — that's all the technical instruction you need. Have fun.

The Peony. This tapestry-like mandala has a subtle ribbon color change to express the shading on the petals of a peony. It was started without a real plan. By the time enough of the central ribbons were in that the six medium pink spokes were established, I realized that with a little planning I could make the illusion of petals, too.

Georgia Peach. The idea was to make a central peach-colored motif
surrounded by green. I constructed it and was displeased. The central
motif seemed too small for the field of green and it just sat there.
Problem: I had only a limited amount of peach-colored ribbon to work
with. Now what? I decided to leave the central peach-colored motif
and one green ribbon, on each of the six sides of the mandala in place.
The next green ribbon out was replaced by a peach-colored ribbon.
Happy days! The mandala and background came into balance with lots of
movement in the outer rings of the mandala.

Passion Flower. This piece was commissioned as a birthday present. It had to be purple. I had some lovely silver and lavender metallic ribbon in my stash along with white, lavender, purple, and, for pop, green satin ribbon. I started building one flower mandala, switched to a green background, and then started a second flower from, the outside in, further down the primary silver ribbons. The third flower grew where the rays of the first two flowers crossed. I just had to fill in the appropriately colored ribbons, mimicking the first flower.

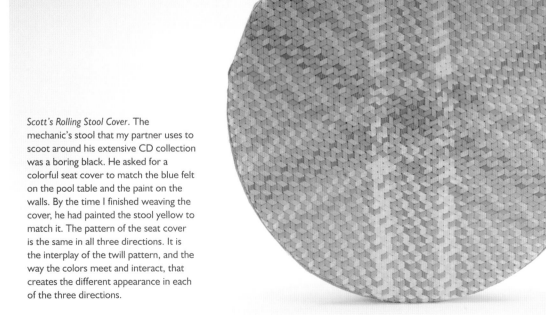

Scott's Rolling Stool Cover. The mechanic's stool that my partner uses to scoot around his extensive CD collection was a boring black. He asked for a colorful seat cover to match the blue felt on the pool table and the paint on the walls. By the time I finished weaving the cover, he had painted the stool yellow to match it. The pattern of the seat cover is the same in all three directions. It is the interplay of the twill pattern, and the way the colors meet and interact, that creates the different appearance in each of the three directions.

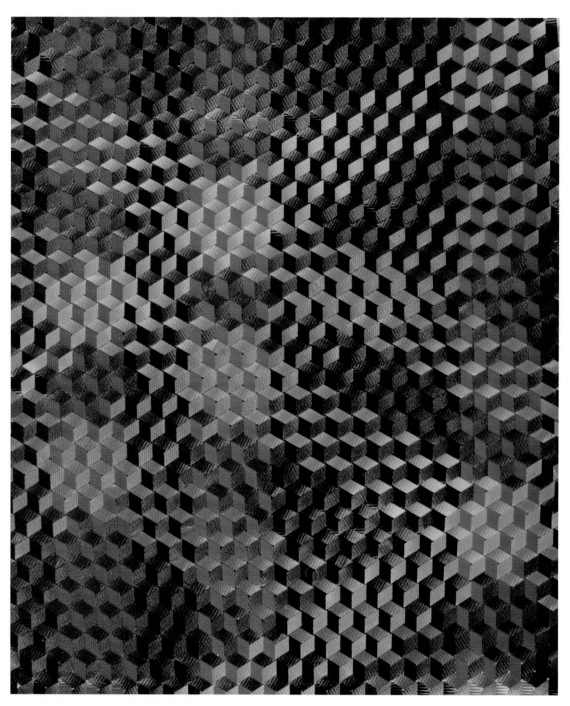

Fireworks. This is a curling ribbon prototype for a wall-hanging to be done in grosgrain ribbon. Fixing the location for each firework so that there would be minimal interaction with each other was more challenging than expected. I ended up starting each mandala independently and then moving them all to one large work surface. Once the approximate positions were decided, they were pinned down and the black-as-night background was woven in.

Star of David. Experiments with different colored ribbons in mad weave will sooner or later start shooting out six-pointed stars. I had it happen often enough that I wanted to do it on purpose. The beautiful gold metallic thread laced with green and red seemed like just the pop the red, green, and gold would need to bring it together. Please note that I broke some rules with this mandala. Because I wanted the points of the star to be nearly solid gold, there are several green ribbons that run below the surface, leaving only two layers of gold showing.

TWILL-BASED MAD WEAVE
11: TAPESTRIES

Tapestry is fabric consisting of a warp upon which colored threads are woven by hand to produce a design, often pictorial, used for wall-hangings, furniture coverings, etc. The inspiration can come from anywhere — and the final product will not necessarily look much like the inspiration.

A mad weave tapestry will most likely be impressionistic if you use one weaver from selvedge to selvedge. Very realistic works can be done with discontinuous wefts. We'll show you some examples of tapestries here and what inspired them. Maybe they will get your creative juices flowing.

Postcard of *Cloudscape – Eastern Shore* by Alvena McCormick and triaxial tapestry *Pink Sunset*. It seemed like such a good idea! There are some of the correct angles that would suggest that a triaxial weave could be developed. I ran the primary layer horizontally and, while that was a good idea, much of the rest did not come together — this time. I keep looking at this postcard and I know I will try again someday. The lesson here is that you shouldn't get discouraged if your project doesn't turn out the way you thought it would. Sometimes, regardless of your experience, you just learn from the first attempt.

Watermelon bag. The inspiration for the watermelon bag was the red ribbon! Who knew? I was buying several spools of curling ribbon for a project when I caught sight of this pink-red ribbon that just screamed watermelon. I promised myself a watermelon-shaped bag. I use it for my knitting bag so that it is always close at hand. It is a great way to show off my mad weave, too!

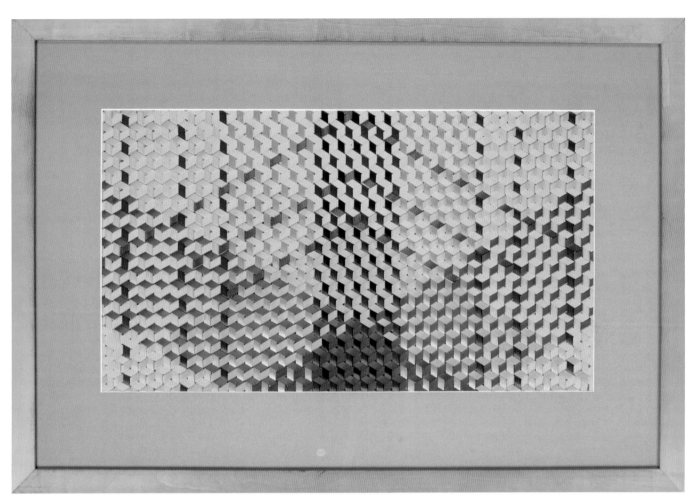

Macon County Library. Framed piece measures 27" x 39". Our county came out with a brochure a few years ago with an artist's rendering of the new library it wanted to build. I had just started doing mad weave at the time, so I saw mad weave in everything — and, sure enough, I saw it in the timber-frame structure of the new building. The actual library has a fireplace centered between the glass doors and I incorporated it into the tapestry that eventually developed from that early inspiration.

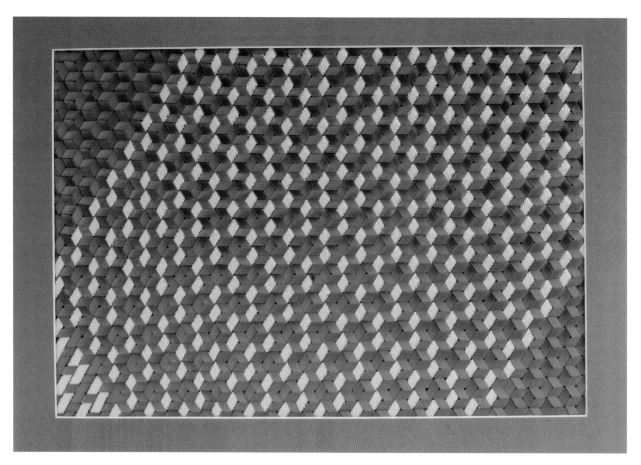

Christmas Gold. Matted piece, 13" x 20". As you started making your first "Stars" pattern, I'm sure you noticed that just two layers created stripes. To me, there were just so many possibilities to consider for the third layer in addition to the stars. I love the star pattern and use it often, but, for a wall-hanging, I wanted to create more interest and movement. Here, I incorporated two different patterns in one piece.

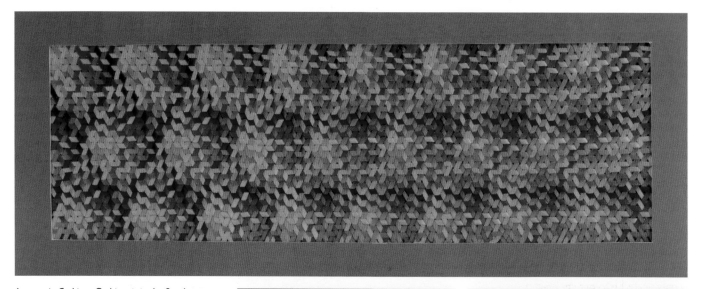

Autumn in Cashiers. Cashiers is in the Smoky Mountains of North Carolina. In 2008, the autumn colors were spectacular — and inspirational. I made several small samplers, *Autumn Prelude I* and *Autumn Prelude II*, trying out the different colors that I was seeing in the trees. Even parts of the actual finished piece were woven and re-woven several times before I finally felt that it represented the foliage I was depicting. Samplers, 5" x 8" each. Matted, it measures out to only 8" x 20".

Autumn Prelude I

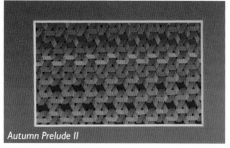

Autumn Prelude II

PROJECTS

▨ SMALL TREASURE BAG

Treasure bags.

Small bags.

These little bags are so handy and such an easy way to carry your mad weave creations with you. They do very well as cases for business cards, as well as a repository for jewelry that is shed as the day goes on. A friend uses one for her rosary. Make a bigger one for a kindle. Consider adding a carrying strap. The list of possibilities is only limited by your imagination.

As you plan your bags, be very generous in sizing them. Allow enough ease to accommodate what you are planning to have reside in the bag. For a business card case-sized bag, make a mad weave fabric that is at least 5" x 8". This size will accommodate a tight 1/2" seam allowance and just enough room for the cards.

Many of the bags pictured are made from .375" width ribbon, but 1/4" ribbon is absolutely marvelous for the business card-size and smaller bags. These bags are all made with the warp ribbon running the long way on the mad weave fabric. There is no reason they couldn't run from side to side, especially if you have a fun novelty ribbon that you want to show off on the flap area only.

Supplies

- RIBBON in .35" or .375" width
- FUSIKNIT® INTERFACING — same size as the mad weave fabric you create
- Piece of LIGHTWEIGHT, COLOR-COORDINATED LINING material the same size as the mad weave fabric
- MATCHING THREAD
- BUTTON, TOGGLE, OR OTHER FASTENER (optional)

Instructions

○ STEP 1: With the weaving complete and ribbons firmly fused to the fusiknit, mark with a pin where you want the fold line for the front flap to be. If you have decided to use a button and loop closure, make the loop now. Cut a piece of ribbon long enough to fit around the button plus .75". Fold the ribbon in half lengthwise and stitch close to the edge. Form the loop and center on the flap edge with all raw edges aligned. Pin securely in place.

○ STEP 2: Cut a liner the same size as the mad weave fabric. Lay mad weaver fabric on liner with right sides facing. (Get in the habit of sewing with the fusiknit side up so that you can see where you are stitching on the ribbons.) Pin the short end that will be the flap edge and stitch. Open and press seam allowance toward the liner. Pin and stitch across the bag 1/4" from the seam that joined the liner to the mad weave fabric. This seam will be visible on the inner flap of the bag and serves to keep the liner in place when the bag is complete.

○ STEP 3: Again, with right sides facing, pin and stitch other short end. (Yes, I know the two pieces don't lay flat against each other any more. It's okay.)

○ STEP 4: Now to sew the sides of the flap, using your pin marker as a guide, pin the side seams of the flap. This seam allowance will be a little less than half an inch. If the warp ribbons run the length of the bag, take care to stitch between the ribbons. When the bag is turned, it makes for a much neater appearance. Stitch from flap edge to marking pin on each side.

○ STEP 5: We don't want any seam allowances to be visible inside or outside the bag, so we must work with the outside of the bag (the mad weave fabric) and the lining separately. To stitch the side seams of the bag, pull the mad weave fabric away from the liner and re-fold so that the portion of fabric that will comprise the

(front and back of the) bag is folded face to face. Pin and stitch both sides starting at the open edge and stitching toward the fold. Again, if the warp ribbons run the length of the bag, take care to stitch between the ribbons. After stitching side seams, I often pull out any ribbons that fall wholly within the seam allowances to reduce the bulk of the seam. Now do the same with the lining EXCEPT that only one side will get machine-stitched. One side will be left open so that the bag can be turned right-side out.

○ STEP 6: Trimming the corners. I do not trim the seam allowances much, if at all. I find that the ribbons ends are much better behaved and are easier to press into submission if left longer.

○ STEP 7: Turn the bag right-side out, working out the corners with the closed point of your shears or some other small blunt object. If you have decided to add a fastener to the bag, do it now before the liner is stitched into place. When you have completed any handwork that you do not want caught in the liner, pull the liner out, fold the seam allowance into place, and blind-stitch closed. Settle the liner into place and press the bag.

Whether used to bring focus to a lovely table display or laid across a piano for a touch of color, a table runner is a wonderful accessory in any room.

This table runner is made from non-directional printed fabric in order to keep the yardage purchased to a minimum. It measures out at 14" wide and 38" long (less than the width of the yardage). It lends itself to endless modifications.

Supplies

- ◆ .25 (or 1/4) yards of 44/45" wide each COTTON PRINT FABRIC in three different but HARMONIZING PRINTS
- ◆ .66 (or 2/3) yards of 44/45" wide COTTON FABRIC OF A SOLID COLOR to harmonize with print fabrics
- ◆ HTC FUSI-KNIT FUSIBLE INTERFACING 10" x 34"
- ◆ SEWING THREAD TO MATCH
- ◆ ROTARY CUTTER AND BOARD
- ◆ STEAM IRON
- ◆ CLOVER TAPE MAKER (optional)

Instructions

◇ STEP 1: Cut eight strips of each print fabric measuring 1-4/5" wide by 44/45" long. Turn the edges of the strips under to form 1"-wide tape using the Clover tape maker. The turned edges are pressed into place using a steam iron. Cut five strips, 1-4/5" wide by 44/45" long of the solid fabric.

◇ STEP 2: Secure the FusiKnit interfacing to the work surface so that it lays at 10" wide and 34" long. Since this is a tumbling block pattern, each layer is a different color. Lay in your first layer of eight strips leaving an inch of fusible interfacing visible on each side. Weave in the second and third layers, covering the interfacing. Make sure everything is aligned properly. This is very important. It is impossible to correct angles once the interfacing is adhered to your mad weave fabric. If your angles are off, when the edging strips are attached to the ends, it will be apparent that the weaving angles are out of alignment. Trim any loose threads and steam-press the fabric to the interfacing. Use a press cloth to preclude catching the tip of the iron on any of the tape strips.

◇ STEP 3: Using the solid-colored strips, edge the mad weave fabric you have created. The side strips will be attached first. The seam line will be just outside the last vertical strip on each side and the finished width should be at approximately 8". Press seam allowances out and away from center panel. Trim off the excess length and use it as the edging of the ends. Pin and baste in place. Fold back and see that you have attached it straight across the woven ends. Stitch in place and press. Cut three strips of the print fabric and apply it as edging, again applying the sides first. Press. Finally, add another edging strip of the solid-color all around. Press.

◇ STEP 4: Cut a piece of the solid-colored fabric to match the size of the finished front panel.

◇ STEP 5: Pin, baste, and sew the front and back panels together, with right sides facing, leaving part of one end open. Turn right-side out and press. Turn seam allowances in at opening and press in place. Sew up the opening neatly and invisibly by hand.

◇ STEP 6: Pin panels together and stitch-in-the-ditch around the center panel to secure the front and back panels together.

PANELED TOTE BAG IN DANCING STAR PATTERN

This colorful, eco-friendly tote bag will gladly tote groceries, your knitting, or the kid's toys. Finished size: 19" wide x 15" tall with 5" bottom pleat. Straps 20".

For those of you who don't like to sew, but like the idea of embellishing a tote bag with mad weave, buy ready-made canvas bags from the craft section of your local department store. Make a mad weave panel or shape and glue it to the bag. Hearts, diamonds, and stars are all easy to make. Use Fray Check® glue to preclude your ribbons from unraveling. Use Ellen's Yes You Can Wash It® glue to stabilize the mad weave and adhere it to the bag.

Supplies

- ◆ RIBBON FOR MAD WEAVE (3 options):
  - a) approximately 36 yards 3/8" grosgrain ribbon
  - b) 27 yards of 1/2" grosgrain ribbon
  - c) 21 yards of 5/8" grosgrain ribbon
- ◆ FusiKnit 11" x 13"
- ◆ 48" of 1" WEBBING for straps
- ◆ 24" of PRE-WASHED STURDY COTTON FABRIC at least 52" wide (sturdy cotton canvas was used here)
- ◆ MATCHING SEWING THREAD

Instructions

◇ STEP 1: Create the mad weave panel for the tote. Pin FusiKnit to your weaving work surface, making sure the rough fusible side is facing up. The Dancing Stars pattern is used here. Instead of using three colors of ribbon, just two were used so that the striped ribbon was showcased. The striped ribbon has asymmetrical stripes. In order to make the pinwheel in the star work properly, the ribbons had to be laid in, similar sides together, for each pair of ribbons. The striped grosgrain ribbon is from Offray and the brown grosgrain is from PaperMart. Importantly, they are both labeled as 5/8" and 3/5", or 15mm, wide. The original ribbon purchased to go with the striped ribbon was a 5/8" red grosgrain that turned out to be only 1/2", or 13mm, wide. It would have worked, but there would be issues with spacing and with keeping all the ribbons aligned to their proper angles. I'll mention the problem, but I won't make you work through it here!

TIPS:

To keep the panel symmetrical, lay in the center striped ribbons first and then work your way to each side. Very important: Work the mad weave pattern to completely cover the FusiKnit. Repeat: Be sure the ends of your ribbons go to the edge of the interfacing! It is very frustrating to get the whole project constructed and have an end of a ribbon pop loose because it wasn't long enough for both corners to catch in the side seam. Use your iron, with a press cloth, to carefully fuse the ribbons all the way to the edges of the interfacing so that no end ribbons can escape the ribbon fabric you have created.

◇ STEP 2: Cut out one panel 20" x 26", one panel 20" x 11", one panel 20" by 4", and two panels 11" x 4". A 1/2" seam allowance is included.

◇ STEP 3: Create center panel. On each side of the mad weave panel, align a 4" x 11" cotton panel face-to-face with the mad weave panel. Pin and stitch. Turn cotton panels out and press. Press all seam allowance out toward the cotton panels. This will allow the ribbons to continue to lay flat. Top stitch seams 1/4" from edge of mad weave panel. Lay this new three part center panel face up on the cotton 20" x 11" panel that you have already cut. Align, pin and baste all edges together.

◇ STEP 4: With right sides facing, align edge of 20" x 4" panel to top edge of center panel. Pin and stitch. With right sides facing, align edge of 20" x 26" panel to bottom edge of center panel. Pin and stitch. Turn both cotton panels out and press flat. Press all seam allowances toward cotton panels. Top stitch these seams from edge to edge and 1/4" from edge of mad weave panel.

◇ STEP 5: Form bag. Fold panel in half width-wise. Align corners. Pin and stitch side seams. Start seam at top of bag and stitch toward fold. Finish edges of seams.

STEPS 1-2

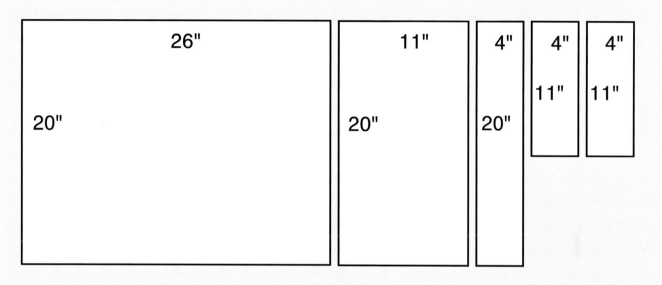

Fabric layout for tote bag.

STEPS 3-4

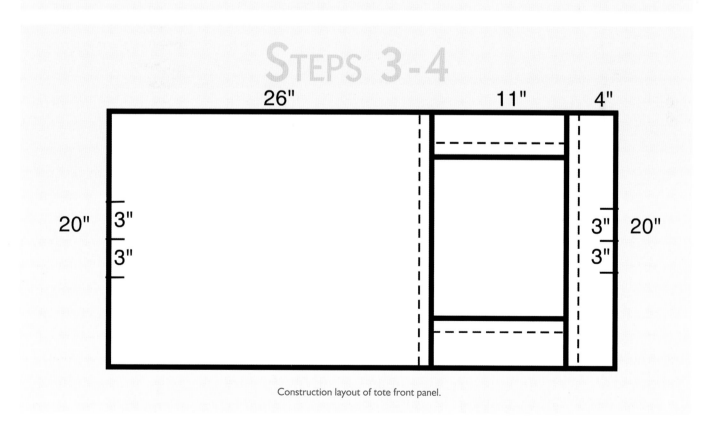

Construction layout of tote front panel.

◇ STEP 6: Form pleat in bottom of bag. With bag wrong-side out, measure 2-1/2" up one side seam, from the bottom fold, and mark with pencil. Fold corner of bag as shown in photo. Make sure fold has positioned the seam straight up the middle. Using the pencil mark as the mid-way point, mark the seam line. The distance from the point of the fold to the end of the seam line should be the same on both sides. Pin and stitch. Repeat on other bottom corner of the bag.

◇ STEP 7: Finish edge and attach handles. With bag wrong side out, fold edge over 1/2" and press. Fold that edge over again, 1" this time, to form hem. Pin and press. Locate and mark the center edge of the front and the back panels. Measure out 3" to either side of center and mark for handle location. Cut the 1" webbing to create two 24" lengths. Insert one end of a handle under the hemline to the outside

of the 3" mark on the front panel. Pin. Insert and secure other end to outside of other 3" mark on the same panel. Repeat instructions to install handle on back panel. Allow handles to hang down out of the way and machine stitch hem in place. Stitch two seams, one at the edge of the hem and one at the edge of the bag. Flip handles up so that they lay across the hem. Stitch the handles in place as pictured. Turn bag right side out and press.

STEPS 5-7

Detail of pleat in bottom of bag.

A look at the detail of the finished hem.

GLASSES CASE

Mad weave fabric used to make glasses cases.

Protect your glasses and show off your mad weave at the same time. Finished size: 6-1/2" x 3-1/4".

Supplies

- Approximately 12 YARDS OF 1/4" RIBBON for mad weave
- Piece of HEAVYWEIGHT INTERFACING 7-1/2" by 7-1/2"
- Piece of FUSIKNIT INTERFACING 7-1/2" by 7-1/2"
- Piece LIGHTWEIGHT LINING MATERIAL, color coordinated with mad weave 7-1/2" by 7-1/2"
- MATCHING THREAD

Instructions

◇ STEP 1: Using a saucer as a guide, round-off one of the corners of the heavyweight interfacing with a pencil. Fold the panel in half with penciled corner on top. Match sides and corners. Pin together. Cut through both layers along pencil line. Round-off the top corners of the liner fabric and the FusiKnit to match the heavyweight interfacing.

◇ STEP 2: Create your case cover. Pin FusiKnit to your weaving work surface. The black and green case is worked in the Dancing Stars pattern with two pieces of shiny narrow ribbon laid in for interest. In the samples, you learned to make the Dancing Stars pattern with three colors. Here, instead of light-, medium-, and dark-colored ribbons there is medium-, medium-, and dark-colored ribbons.

The other case is worked in the Spot Pattern. Instead of using one color for the spots, different shades of blue, in a gentle gradation, were used in all three directions. Work the mad weave pattern of your choice to cover the FusiKnit. **Very Important:** Be sure the ends of your ribbons go to the edge of the interfacing! It would be frustrating to complete your project and have corners of ribbons sticking out because the ribbon was not long enough for all the corners to catch in the seams. Use your iron to fuse the ribbons to the interfacing. Remember that any inlaid narrow ribbons don't touch the interfacing. Secure them with pins until the ribbon fabric you have created is sewn to the lining.

◇ STEP 3: Place liner fabric and mad weave cover together, right sides facing. Align rounded corners. Pin, baste, and stitch around the edges, leaving the bottom edge open. Clip curve to seam line and trim corners and edges as necessary. Turn case right side out. Press.

◇ STEP 4: Trim piece of interfacing until it fits inside the case between the lining and the case cover. Turn in the raw edges of the case cover and lining. Press, pin and use whip-stitch to close.

◇ STEP 5: Fold case in half lengthwise, right-side out. Align and pin. Tack the two layers together, placing tacks inconspicuously between ribbons. Place tacks across bottom and up side of case, stopping just short of corner curve.

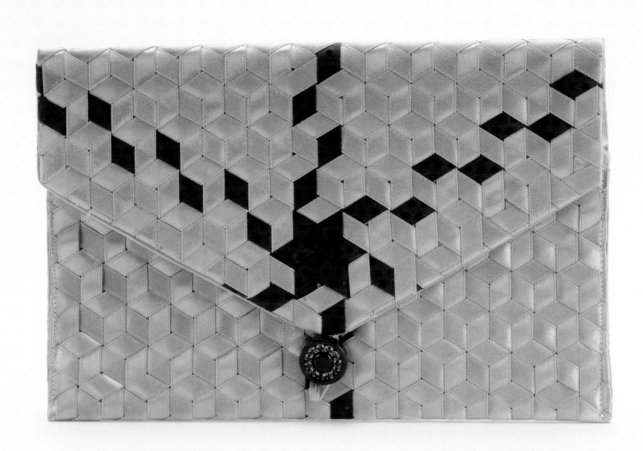

This elegant bag travels well and is big enough to hold all your essentials for an evening out. Finished size: 7" x 10".

Supplies

- ◆ APPROXIMATELY 33 YARDS OF .375" RIBBON IN MAIN COLOR
- ◆ NEARLY 3 YARDS OF .375" RIBBON IN CONTRASTING COLOR
- ◆ Piece of HEAVYWEIGHT INTERFACING as used for handbags 10" x 7"
- ◆ Piece of FUSIKNIT INTERFACING 12" x 18"
- ◆ Piece of LIGHTWEIGHT LINING MATERIAL, color coordinated with mad weave 18" x 12"
- ◆ MATCHING THREAD
- ◆ FANCY BUTTON

To maintain its shape, the back panel of the bag is stiffened with a piece of the very heavyweight interfacing used for handbags. Medium-weight cardboard could also be used. The softness of the woven fabric is preserved in the front panel and flap. If a firmer bag is preferred, cut a piece of interfacing for each panel.

Instructions

○ STEP 1: Although not strictly required, draw an 18" x 12" rectangle on the work surface. Extend the center line that runs lengthwise on the board so that it is visible past the edges of the rectangle. Mark the angle lines so that they also extend past the edges of the rectangle. Especially when using black fusiknit, the lines are difficult to see within the work area and reference lines are particularly important here because they will define the leading edge of the flap. Place these two reference lines so that they converge, crossing the center line, approximately 1/2" inside the rectangle perimeter. (That leaves room for the seam allowance.) Pin the FusiKnit to the work surface, sticky (rough) side up.

With the Star pattern, it is easiest to start by placing the two contrasting color ribbons up either side of the center line and then one ribbon of the main color on each side, giving four warp ribbons to work within establishing the weaving pattern. There are two main color ribbons along the flap edge and two contrasting color ribbons for the pattern. The rest of the piece is in the main color. After the star pattern is established, lay in the rest of the warp ribbons. There are eleven main color ribbons to either side of the center two ribbons. Note that they only need to extend about 1/2" past the flap edges (seam allowance) and do not need to go all the way to the edge of the rectangle. These ribbons will establish the width of the bag. Weave in the remainder of the weft ribbons. Also note that there is top stitching along the sides of the bag. Lay in the weft ribbons with tails extending out past the last warp ribbon on each side to allow for the seam allowance and top stitching. If in doubt, go all the way to the edge of the FusiKnit. Check for weaving errors. Press.

○ STEP 2: Based on the size of the button, cut a piece of ribbon to be used for the loop. The loop should be long enough to fit around the button, plus 3/4" extra for seam allowance. Press the ribbon in half lengthwise and stitch along the edge. Pin in place as pictured.

○ STEP 3: With right sides together, pin the woven material to the lining. Be sure the loop is aligned properly. The stitch line along the flap will be just outside the last weft ribbons. After stitching the flap seams, stitch straight across the point of the flap to firmly secure the loop and the point ribbons. On the side seams, place the seam line about 1/4" outside of the last ribbon. Trim corners. Turn and press the bag. Leave the bottom open.

○ STEP 4: Fold the bag to its final shape. Decide how big the flap will be. Cut the heavyweight interfacing to fit inside the back panel and then trim another 1/2" off the width. Slide it into place. Turn in the bottom seam allowances and pin firmly in place. Top stitch a 1/4" from edge. Determine button placement and secure button in place. Fold bag and pin side seams in place. The interfacing was cut so that it could be manipulated out of the way when making the top stitched seams. Tap the edge of the bag to get the interfacing to move out of the way of the stitch line. When one side is done, move the interfacing out of the way and do the second side. Pull ends of threads to one side and tie off before clipping.

STEP 2

Bag detail

102

These pillows, made from gradated color fabric, make wonderful visual focal points for a chair, bed, or even a room. Each pillow will finish out at 18+" square.

Supplies

- 1-3/4 yards of 44/45" wide COTTON FABRIC that graduates in color from edges to center
- 20" square of COLOR COORDINATED COTTON MATERIAL for back of pillow
- 18" x 20" square of FusiKnit FUSIBLE INTERFACING
- 20" square of MUSLIN for backing

- 18" square of FUSIBLE FLEECE INTERFACING
- BAG OF FIBERFILL OR 18" PILLOW FORM
- SEWING THREAD TO MATCH
- ROTARY CUTTER AND BOARD
- STEAM IRON
- CLOVER TAPE MAKER (optional)

Instructions

- STEP 1: Cut all of gradated fabric into 1-4/5" wide strips. Be sure to cut the strips straight across the fabric so that the full length of the gradation is in each 44/45" long strip. This is where using the Clover tape maker really comes in handy. Use it to turn the edges of the strips under to form 1"-wide tape. The turned edges are pressed into place using a steam iron. Turn all of the strips but two. These pieces will be used to edge the pillow front. Cut all of the long strips/tapes in half forming 22" long strips.

- STEP 2: Secure the FusiKnit interfacing to the work surface so that it lays at 18" wide and 20" long. Lay in your first layer with dark-colored ends to the top. Lay in enough strips to almost cover the width of the interfacing. The strips will overhang the interfacing, top and bottom, by about an inch. The second and third layers are laid in with the dark-colored ends to the left side. The ends of the strips should extend out far enough to cover the interfacing. The resulting color pattern is all dark in the top left corner and all light in the lower right-hand corner, with mixed light and dark in the other two corners.

- STEP 3: Now, take the two unpressed strips and cut them in half if you have not already done so. These will be used to edge the front of the pillow. The side strips will be attached first. Align the color gradations the same way the weaving was laid in. The seam line will be just outside the last vertical strip on each side and the finished width should be at approximately 18". If you have chosen to keep the pillow square, lay the end edging pieces the same distance apart as the side edging pieces. Pin and baste in place. Fold back and see that you have attached it straight across the woven ends. Stitch in place. Baste the muslin lining to the back of the mad weave fabric you have created.

- STEP 4: Center the fusible fleece lining to the center of the fabric you have chosen for the back of the pillow and fuse into place.

- STEP 5: Pin, baste, and sew the front and back sections together, with right sides facing and leaving part of one side open. Turn right-side out and press. Turn seam allowances in at opening and press in place. Stuff pillow with fiberfill and sew up the opening neatly and invisibly by hand.

IMPORTANT:

Make sure everything is aligned properly. It is impossible to correct angles once the interfacing is adhered to your mad weave fabric. If your angles are off, when the edging strips are attached to the ends, it will be apparent that the weaving angles are out of alignment. The edging strips will not appear to be squarely applied. Trim any loose threads and steam-press the fabric to the interfacing. Use a press cloth to prevent catching the tip of the iron on any of the tape strips.

CONCLUSION

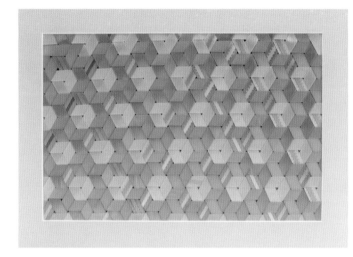

Pastel spots tapestry

Lavender Fields

There is so much room for creativity in triaxial weaving! We are pleased to present two new ways to weave hex weave and mad weave that make these fascinating structures more accessible and easier to use and to teach. We have given you the tools. Now we encourage you to break the rules. Deviate from the patterns. Lay in supplemental ribbons. Use two weavers side-by-side for pinwheel effects. Pin findings all over the place. Embellish with pearls or beads at every intersection of the ribbons. Feed yarn, string, or cord from intersection to intersection. Change color in the middle of a layer. Introduce new colors on each layer. The book is full of pieces where we have done some or all of the above. Don't feel constrained to do just what we did: explore, imagine, and make each triaxial weaving you create your own.

Two artists who'd taught quite a few
Were determined to try something new.
What a good time they had,
Making every one Mad,
And were carried off shouting "Yahoo!"

TROUBLESHOOTING
HEX-DERIVED MAD WEAVE

If something in your weaving looks wrong to you, you are probably right. Mistakes are inevitable, but how to find them? They tend to proliferate so that many strips may be affected by a single error. Fortunately, once you have found errors, many of them can be corrected. Most of the errors in mad weave appear when you are lashing the first two layers together.

Problem: You cannot merge the two layers of hex weave.

It is likely that you are trying to combine a right-handed hex and a left-handed hex. You will either have to reweave one of the hexes or, better yet, make two new hexes, one right-handed and one left-handed, to complete the original mismatched pair. Finish them off and you will have two mad weaves!

Problem: An expected pattern is appearing only intermittently.

This could be a weaving error — it is easy to pick up or drop a strip, and "over 2, under 3" can become "over 3, under 2."

It could also be that you have a mistake in the color sequence you originally set up. Check your pattern colors.

Problem: There is a ladder of mistakes that runs through an entire column.

You have probably left out a strip in lashing the two hexes together. Since the pattern of a row is the same as the row three rows below (and three rows above), you can find the missing row by scanning across your piece. There are three strip patterns, and each corresponds to only one group of strips. All "row ones" will have the same pattern and all "row twos" will have the same pattern, but a pattern that is different from the one in row one. So, while counting "pattern one, pattern two, pattern three," it is relatively easy to find the missing column.

Problem: The strips will not slide into place.

When one strip is blocked by another, you have either made a weaving error or you are trying to combine a right-handed hex with a left-handed hex.

Problem: The edge strips keep loosening and falling out.

This happens, especially with slippery materials. Try pinning the edges to the work surface.

Search Strategies

Sometimes it can be really difficult to find mistakes. Here are the tricks we use in addition to the troubleshooting suggestions above:

◯ Turn the piece over — it is often easier to see irregularities if you get another view.

◯ Turn the piece sideways.

◯ Scan down individual strips to see that each strip alternates "over 2, under 3" or "over 3, under 3," depending on which level you are on.

◯ Check that all your diamonds are touching at their long ends (see "Diamonds are a girl's best friend," Chapter 7).

◯ Check for irregularities in the built-in stars. All complete mad weaves have small six-strip pinwheels. Your color design will make the pinwheels more or less apparent. If they are easy to find, check each one to find the one(s) that are not properly formed.

◯ Check for irregularities in the defining triangles. Each time the three weaving elements (horizontal strips, left-pointing strips, and right-pointing strips) intersect, they form a small triangle. All of the triangles should show the same woven pattern.

◯ Finally, the most powerful search strategy is to scan the diamonds. They should be parallelograms, not trapezoids. The only places where you should have trapezoids are at the edges of the figure, where some mad weave units will not be completed.

ANGLE GUIDES AND GRAPH PAPER

We have included two angle guides. They both do the same things, but they vary enough that you will probably have a preference and useful enough that you will want to use them. Feel free to copy them at whatever scale you would like. You might want to copy them on clear plastic so that you can see through them or draw one on your work surface.

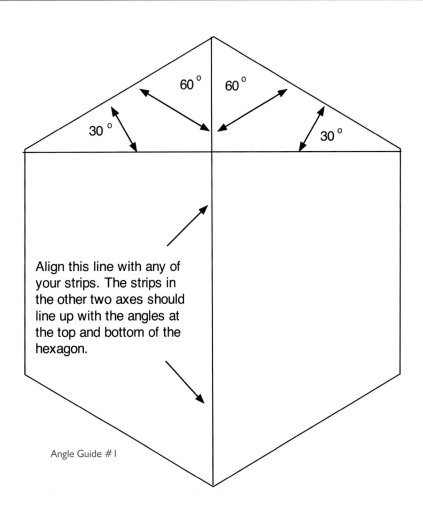

60° 60°

30° 30°

Align this line with any of your strips. The strips in the other two axes should line up with the angles at the top and bottom of the hexagon.

Angle Guide #1

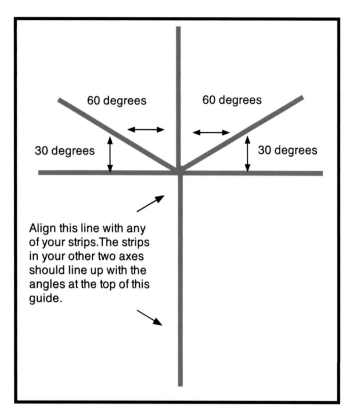

60 degrees   60 degrees

30 degrees   30 degrees

Align this line with any of your strips. The strips in your other two axes should line up with the angles at the top of this guide.

Angle Guide #2

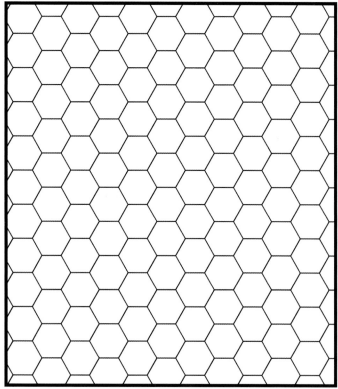

Hexagonal graph paper

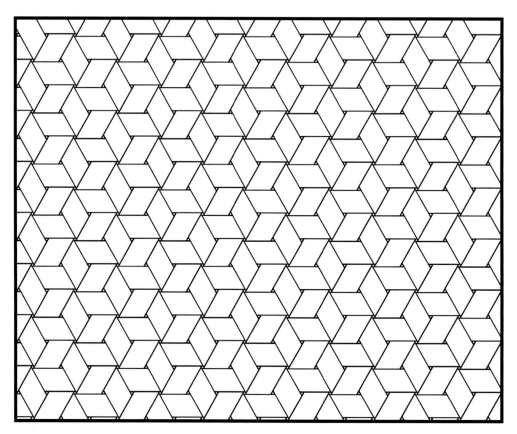

Mad weave graph paper

MAD WEAVE PATTERN LIBRARY (FOR TWILL-BASED MAD WEAVE)

See Chapter Seven for hex-based mad weave patterns. When you are weaving hex-based mad weave, you are working with all of the strips in a given layer, but when you are working with the twill-based method, you are working with all the strips in a single direction. The instructions are very different.

- Tumbling blocks: different color in each layer

- Spots: (dark) — 2 light, 1 dark each layer

- Stacked Spots: 1 dark, 1 medium, 1 light each layer

- Stars: (light) — 1 dark, 2 light each layer

- Dancing Stars: 2 light, 2 medium, 2 dark each layer

- Pinwheels: think old quilt pattern — 1 light, 1 dark each layer

- Stripes: (light) — variation on stars — 2 light, 1 dark on two layers, all light on one layer

- Tiaras: variation on stacked spots — 1 dark, 1 medium, 1 light each layer

- Field of Stars: variation on dancing stars — 2 light, 4 dark each layer

- Strings of Diamonds: (light) — two layers dark, one layer light

- Quilting Roses: 3 dark, 3 medium, 3 light each layer (cluster of 3 same-colored-strips in center, all layers)

- Pinwheel Roses: 3 dark, 3 medium, 3 light each layer (one spot in center when light color is to one side of center and medium color is on the other side of center on all layers)

MADWEAVER

Richard Harris, the husband of co-author Elizabeth Harris, has been working on a drawdown program called MadWeaver, which helps design mad weaves. Many of the drawings in this book were produced using MadWeaver. There are a lot of features on this page. MadWeaver is a continuously-evolving application on the website: www.fiberwoman.com/madweave/madweave.html

- Use up to six colors in a single design

- Control the hue, value, saturation, and transparency of each color

- Use up to 24 strips per direction

- Add one strip at a time to build your own design or modify any of the five built-in patterns

- Hide the buttons so that you save only the mad weave image

- Save as an .svg or .png image

- Create a right- or left-pointing mad weave

- Outline the strips or not

- Four densities let you control how tightly the strips are woven

- Show or hide each direction independently

- Show or hide each layer independently

- Remove strips by making them transparent

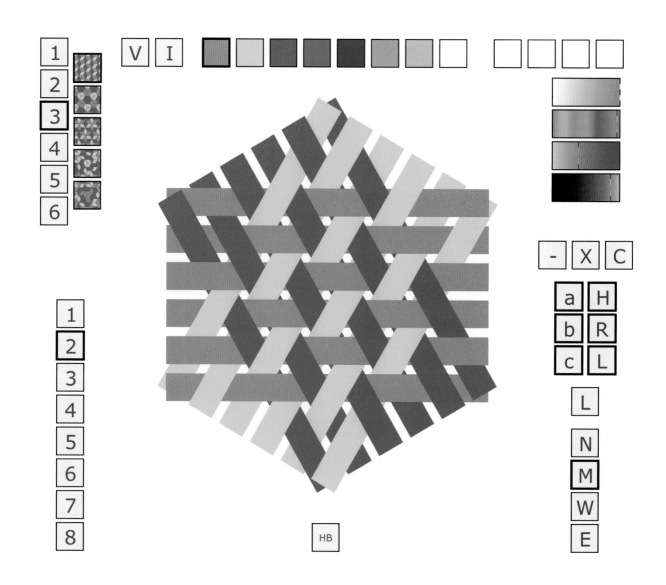

This is an example of what can be done on the Mad Weaver website. The possibilities are endless!

BIBLIOGRAPHY & RESOURCES

BIBLIOGRAPHY

Blake, Kathy. *Handmade Books: A Step-by-Step to Crafting Your Own Books.* Boston, Massachusetts: Little Brown and Company, 1997.

Boles, Martha, and Rochelle Newman. *The Surface Plane.* Bradford, Massachusetts: Pythagorean Press, Brown and Benchmark Publishers, 1992.

Gerdes, Paulus. *Geometry from Africa, Mathematical and Educational Explorations.* Washington, D.C.: The Mathematical Association of America, 1999.

Harvey, Virginia L. *The Techniques of Basketry.* Seattle, Washington: University of Washington, 1988.

Lang-Harris, Elizabeth. *An Introduction to Triaxial Weaving.* Suwanee, Georgia: Handweavers Guild of America, Shuttle, Spindle, and DyePot, Volume 39, Issue 153, 48-52.

LaPlantz, Shereen. *The Mad Weave Book.* Bayside, California: Press De LaPlantz, 1984.

Mooney, David R. *Braiding Triaxial Weaves: Enhancements and Design for Artworks.* Ars Tetrina 5, 1986; pp. 9-31. *Handweaving Triaxial Weaves with Braiding Techniques: Triaxial Braiding.* Ars Tetrina 3, 1985; 99-124.

Shore, Sally. *A Ribbon Weaver's Handook,* Locust Valley, New York: Self-published, 2008.

RESOURCES

(The authors have done business with each of the sites highlighted here and have been pleased with all of them.)

Wood Boxes: AFTOSA (www.aftosa.com) — I often mount my small pieces in wood boxes that are made for showcasing pottery tiles. There's a depression in the center of the box into which a tile can be glued — or you can substitute a triaxial weave of tile size, either four and a quarter inches or six inches square.

Clock Parts: CLOCK PARTS.COM (www.ClockParts.com) and KLOCKIT (www.Klockit.com)

Veneer Inlays: ACUTE MARQUETRY AND DESIGN (www.acutemarquetry.com) and INLAY PRODUCT WORLD, INC. (www.inlays.com)

ACKNOWLEDGMENTS

I would like to thank the many people who have made this book a reality. First, thank you to my friends and family, who overlooked broken dates, forgotten birthdays, and phone calls that had to wait until I was finished with the next piece in this wonderful puzzle.

Thanks also to the Basketry Guild of the Lexington Society of Arts and Crafts, especially Lois Russell, Judy Olney, and Marge Weerts, each of them superb basket weavers and teachers, who introduced me to Hex Weave, and then to Mad Weave, and have cheered me on at every crossing.

The staff at Schiffer Publishing has been universally supportive. Our editor, Nancy Schiffer, is there when we need her, warm and assuring, but not intrusive. Doug Congdon-Martin, who took many of the photographs and made us look good. Also, thank you to Stephanie Daugherty, an excellent spinner and weaver, for introducing me to Nancy Schiffer.

Thanks to the Handweavers' Guild of America, especially Sandy Bowles, for asking me to participate in the Shuttle, Spindle, and Dyepot Learning Exchange, where I met Charlene and had a great class in which I actually learned to weave Mad Weave over the Internet.

Hat's off to my students over the past ten years — thank you for teaching me how to teach triaxial weaving and for asking the right questions that sent me back to my weaving to learn more.

Thanks to Charlene, who never doubted that we had a contribution to make.

Special thanks to my husband, Richard Harris, who ran the house, cooked the meals, wrote a computer program that we used to generate mad weave drawdowns, and wrestled with two computers that were not totally compatible, while I wrestled with bull's eyes and color placement. Rick, you're the greatest!

And finally, to my father, Morris Weiss, for teaching me two of the most powerful words in any language, "What if...?"

I give special thanks to Gail Griffith. Her willingness to teach what she knew of triaxial weaving at the Western North Carolina Fiber and Handweavers Guild Fall Retreat several years ago finally launched me on this mad path. Her encouragement through the years has been a precious gift.

Don Long, tailor and adviser extraordinaire, has been there for me when I didn't have time to look at my sewing machine, much less sit down and use it. His work on the tote bag and pillows is gratefully acknowledged.

Pat and Jim Zilbauer and Pat Gibbs at Sew Creative Sewing and Quilt Shop, Franklin, North Carolina, for making such beautiful fabric available — and even more thanks for the advice, unstintingly given, on fabric selection, sewing supplies, and creating quilts.

Elizabeth, who started out as my mentor in the HGA Learning Exchange, became my dear friend, and always treated me as her equal.

For all the people who ooo-ed and aaah-ed at the appropriate time or inquired after the book's progress, with great goodwill, I say thank you.

Elizabeth Lang-Harris

Charlene St. John